All Alone on the 68th Floor

How one Woman Changed the Face of Construction

Barbara A. Res

Copyright Barbara A. Res
All Rights Reserved
July 2013

2nd Edition

This book is dedicated to my husband, Peter Res

CONTENTS

Introduction 7

Chapter 1 - My Beginnings 16

Chapter 2 - Becoming an Engineer 41

Chapter 3 - The Real World 61

Chapter 4 - The Field 76

Chapter 5 - The Hyatt - Be Careful What You Wish For 83

Chapter 6 - A Position of Authority 99

Chapter 7 - Trump Tower, A Position of Respect 110

Chapter 8 - Construction Manager to the Stars 137

Chapter 9 - The World Meets Trump Tower 151

Chapter 10 - The Other Real World 188

Chapter 11 - Back Where I Belong	201
Chapter 12 - The Plaza	218
Chapter 13 - Two Failures	239
Chapter 14 – Transitions	255
Chapter 15 - My Epiphany	261
Chapter 16 - The Best Job I Never Had	281
Epilogue	292
Acknowledgements	303

INTRODUCTION

For most of my working life, people have called me a pioneer. So, I looked it up. Merriam Webster Dictionary definition of pioneer: a person or group that originates or helps open up a new line of thought or activity or a new method or technical development. Is that me?

In the year 1972, when I graduated from engineering school, the percentage of females wasn't even worth measuring, at less than 1%. I was one of 3 in a class of 800. I started working in the construction business in New York City, and the number of women I encountered was exactly zero.

By the 1980s, the number of female engineers graduating from college had started rising and, by the turn of the century, it was near 20%. It held steady for a while, and then, started dropping. The percentage of female graduates in engineering in 2011 hit a 15 year low at under 18%. What's the phenomenon here? Can part of it be that women stay away from the field because they know that female engineers do not get promoted? Or is it that it is just too damned hard? Are women afraid? Maybe, the price is simply too high for most females. Or, maybe, they actually believe the hype. How many times do you need to be told you can't do math and science before you start believing it?

In 2010, women held 24% of the nation's jobs in all science, technology, engineering, and Math fields. They earned 86 cents for every dollar a man earned. In 2011, women held only 6.3% of the top positions. One can argue that women do much better in the sciences, given that in Industry, as a whole, women fare even worse. Of the 500 largest companies in all industries, women hold only 3% of the top management positions. That's less than half the number of women with top jobs in science and engineering. Why the disparity? My theory is that women who even enter the sciences professionally have already overcome hurdles, which weeded out all but the strongest candidates. Therefore, in the science heavy fields, the female candidate, on average, is going to be superior to her male counterpart who did not face and overcome the same challenges.

Nevertheless, whether it is 3% or 6%, women do not occupy anything close to the 51% of the population that American women comprise in top positions. The fact remains that, in all industries, women hit the same glass ceiling and, in construction, they hit a brick wall as well.

Statistics support sentiments in the popular culture. Consider recent remarks like presidential candidate Rick Santorum's 2012 comment that women should not be allowed to participate in combat because the men they are fighting with will be distracted, and missions jeopardized. And former Harvard University President Lawrence Summer's comment that there are fewer women in engineering and the sciences because they do not have the same aptitude for these subjects. The fact is that women who are not in combat don't become generals. And if the dean thinks you have an inferior intellect, it's not likely you will department head any time soon. The prophesies fulfill themselves. And they work as well today, if not as obviously, as they did 40 years ago when they were leveled at me.

The Construction Industry does not lead the field in employment of female engineers, architects and engineers, but many have made inroads into the main office, since my day. There are project managers, real estate and development executives, financial officers, etc. However, the number of women actually working in the construction trades with tools, or as supervisors of men in the field has grown at a much slower rate, dismally less than those in office management roles. The bottom line is that the money is in the field, and everyone knows this. A skilled laborer makes more than an architect, just like a mechanic makes more than a nurse. For now, the field work is for the men. Relating back to the self-fulfilling prophesy, it is very hard to become the president or CEO of a construction company unless you have worked in the field, much the same as combat. The field is not supplying a pool of women for high management positions. In fact, almost all of the women who are in top positions in the Industry come from Sales, Marketing, Accounting, and Law. Not Engineering.

When I was a draftsman at Zwicker Electric, the men said there would never be a female electrician because a woman could not hump pipe. (that means carry). Oh, they got great enjoyment out of rubbing that in my face, especially since they obviously couldn't claim a woman can't be an electrical engineer any more – I was one! Plus, they just liked using the word "hump" around me. Well, there may be truth to the assumption that fewer women than men can carry extremely heavy articles but brute strength is not and never was important to being an electrician. The guys that end up humping pipe are the ones best suited to the chore. Wiring control boxes with hundreds of terminations requires incredible dexterity and small hands.

Yet, these ridiculous "strength" arguments successfully kept women out of several fields such as police work for many years beyond the women's equality movement. It took a disparate impact suit to get the NYC police department to drop height and weight requirements. And it was only 1982, when the NYC fire department was forced to change the official name for a person who puts out fires to fire*fighter* from fire*man*, when they finally allowed women in the ranks, having their pretextural requirements also summarily eliminated by the courts. It is important to know that when the typing machine was invented, only men were able to become typewriters. Considered a very masculine occupation, it was thought scandalous for a women to even think of doing such a thing. When women started doing the work, the official name of the occupation became typist.

While I was making my way up the ranks in management, not one single woman came across my path in the trades until around 1979.

That woman was a tin knocker, whom I met when I was working on the Hyatt. (By the way, she was terrific – which just goes to support my comment about the need to excel.) Today the government estimates say that somewhere around 5% of construction jobs are filled by females even though there are now laws against discrimination, as well as "sexual harassment" and there are no longer pornographic pictures lining the walls, an "in your face" deterrent. (Anecdotally, according to Industry insiders, this number appears to be closer to 3%.) Why is that number so low? Is it because there is still sufficient harassment and discrimination to deter women? The percentage of women in apprentice ship classes far outnumber the percentage of women on the job. In fact, many women quit. Could it also be that women are afraid to take these jobs because they really believe they are not fit to do them? After all, "Tonka trucks are built tough for boys." That's what they say – and many people believe. There is men's work and women's work. Are schools actively directing girls to shop and boys to home economics? What has really changed? How many Foremen are Fore*women*? The answer is too few to count.

You would think the ridiculous ideas of 1972 have found a resting place, and you would be wrong. I was amazed recently to see an ad for a mechanical superintendent, which is a high level field management job and has nothing to do with manual labor. In the advertisement it said the candidate "must be able to lift and move up to 75 pounds". This was a national construction company, a household name. When I told my husband about this ad, he was shocked, and disgusted. He was there when the men at Zwicker gave me a hard time. We both know the beast when we see it. This ad reeks of discrimination. Its impact is hardly different from what, in my day, would have been listed as "employment – male". In 2012 terms, it is a blatant attempt to discourage women from applying for a position the contractors *prefer* giving to a man. Because they want to keep women out of the field. The field is just another version of the old boy's club. I was a mechanical superintendent in my career, one of the best, I was told. I did that job, and I never moved or lifted a goddamned thing. I can tell you that in a year on the job, I didn't have to do the physical work an average nurse does in an ordinary day. Yet, if I applied for this job today, I would have to do lie on the application, because I cannot lift 75 pounds or anything close.

Meanwhile, the women who *do* work in construction report more incidents of sexual harassment than any other field except mining. Over half of women in construction have been fondled, touched or propositioned. Many report being victims of accidents and tricks. The same kinds of experiences I endured 40 years ago. It is understandable then that there are so few women who are willing to subject themselves to the abuse and hardship of trying to do a job at which they can and should be able to excel. They are sabotaged, there is no female leadership, and they are forced to submit to gender stereotypes. The women who do this work are, in many ways, pioneers themselves.

I did a job when there were no women doing it. I attained a level of success and looked back to see there were very few women behind me. The few women who were there were in the trades, and they did not bond with me, they kept out of the mix, trying to sneak by under the radar. There is no feminism in construction, the women I met particularly eschewed it. I tried to encourage these few and I was rebuffed. These women prefer to be individuals, each acting as one of the boys. This mentality is defensive and it will not change until we stop defining occupations by gender.

So, yes, I am a Pioneer. I accept the title and embrace the responsibility that inures to the role. I will continue to lead the way for other women and for men who are interested in equal treatment and making the most out of our country's labor force, and this book is a major element of that effort.

To this I add just a few words:

Here is something I tell my daughter and her friends. Your grandmother was born without the right to vote. That puts things into perspective for them, immediately. It's really important for young women to understand this. It is important for them to look into the history of the questionable claims and specious excuses that have enabled men, and even our own government, to systematically deprive women of their rights, and to realize that the practice continues to this day, on many levels. Equal Employment is at the very heart of equal rights, you cannot have one without the other. It is important for all Americans to understand that the only requisite to being able to do a job is ability. And that doing a particular job is not a reflection on the nature or character of the worker doing it. Nowhere is this more apparent than in construction, where the work and anyone who does it is considered masculine. Choice empowers. Women are being denied the opportunity to participate in construction and disparaged if they dare to try. Women can only change this by rejecting the stereotypes.

"I define my work, it does not define me," is a conviction essential to any woman who chooses to stray beyond the world of the pink collar. It is not about trying to do a man's job by thinking like a man, it is about doing any job with the confidence that you can be yourself and succeed as such.

In the following pages I will share my experiences as a woman working in what I like to call the last bastion of male supremacy – the construction business. I hope the hardships and rewards of my journey will provide some inspiration and shine a light on a subject that is not often examined, but deserves to be.

If you happened to be reading the newspaper in Boca Raton, on Christmas Day, 1980, you might have seen the headline, "Woman engineer may be first in nation to build skyscraper." That was me and the skyscraper was Trump Tower. How did I get to there, and why did I do it? Why did I subject myself to harassment, humiliation, discrimination, - for the validation of seeing my name in print? What was left of the real me by the time I became Executive Vice President of the Trump Organization? What good did any of this do? What is there about me that even made me try? Has it been worth it?

Chapter 1 - My Beginnings

I was born in Brooklyn, New York, in 1949. My family was poor. Maybe, working class. Or from a socioeconomic viewpoint, low class. Of course, we didn't really think we were low class because everyone else on the block was the same. Some had better cars, more clothes, but, far and wide, we were all the same. And the world was so big then, we didn't really have much exposure to power or wealth. Our family of five lived in a one bedroom apartment in Bay Ridge. There was a great vacant lot across the street. My earliest memory is not so early, I was about 4. I remember someone saying what a cute little girl I was and me crying because I said I wasn't a girl, I was a boy. The reason for this was most of the kids were boys and I wanted to play with them. Lots of times I came across the no girls allowed mantra and, early in life, I learned that it was better to be a boy. Plus I did not play with dolls. I had them, but I didn't like them at all. I preferred animals, stuffed and alive.

When I was 5, we moved into a very small house. There were lots more kids on the street and I started hanging out with girls. We mostly skated, and played jump rope. The boys and girls played together. I went to kindergarten in public school because I was too young for the Catholic school. Then I did 6 months more of kindergarten at Our Lady of Angels. I loved school from the start, going to school in the day, and then playing school when I wasn't outside. I used to do reading with my classmates in learning groups and it was a great experience. This was before homogeneous groupings, which destroyed early education in my mind. I was a popular, skinny kid that did very well in school. And I sang in shows. I once went to a nun's convention dressed up in the full garb, and I was asked to sing. What a sight, a three foot tall Sister of Charity plugging out R&B classics in full voice.

I had a problem with two kids, Billy and Mary Ellen, who I walked to school with every day. Once we got far enough from home they would beat me up. This happened virtually every day. One kid would hold me up and the other would punch me in the stomach. Finally, I told my mother and she reported the kids to the school and it stopped – just like that. But what is amazing is that I took it for so long. This would happen again in my life.

When I was 7 years old I fell on my head. I was climbing on the banister of a high stoop pretending I was a circus performer and I just fell. It was about 12 feet and I hit the sidewalk headfirst and was knocked out. My mother who was across the street came running over and saw me and turned to stone. She could not move. Someone picked me up and carried me to my house. The doctor came and told my mother I had a brain concussion. He said I would come to, and be OK, but she should keep me home from school for a week. I lost a lot of time from school that year, so much so that I did not get any grades for a whole semester. I always thought that fall on the head was lucky for me. While I was home, the class sent me a basket of candy and toys, comic books, coloring books and crayons. That was the greatest present. I was really loved in that school because I was such a good student and helped the other kids out.

We lived about three blocks from the school and we walked all the time. I used to walk to Novena with the kids on the block. We really had a tremendous amount of freedom given we were so little. In the summer, we all went to arts and crafts at the local public school. We stayed there all day so we called it summer school. At the end of the summer they had a talent show and I sang three songs, all by myself. It was *Chances Are* and *The Twelfth of Never* as sung by Johnny Mathis and *The Wayward Wind*. They were giant hits and I was a big hit with the 300 or so mothers and kids in the audience. This was a very good year for me. Then we moved to Queens.

This move changed me. The new kids were good but very different from the ones in Brooklyn, for instance they didn't know from skating or bottle caps. My old friends were in larger groups with older kids too. In Queens, there were just a few kids and all we did was sit on stoops or walk to the candy store. We played board games, not street games. I was used to a lot of activity, here is was just hanging around. I got fairly fat, until I finally got a bicycle when I was 11 or 12 and I when I got more active I started dropping the pounds.

Richie Long was the wealthiest kid in our town. He had a birthday party at a movie, with ice cream at Jahn's, the most famous ice-cream parlor in NY City. This party was a legend in Ozone Park. Question: why are rich kids commonly called Rich? Is this just another cruelty of nature that every time we call out his name we have to be reminded of his wealth? Well, of all natural cruelties, the worst was I was sick the day of the party. They went to a movie about a circus. The whole gang but me. Then to the greatest ice cream parlor in the world. Home of the "kitchen sink." Anyway, Richie's mom brought me some ice cream at home.

This kind of just missing out turned out to be a pattern in my life. I never got that brass ring, somehow. Always came close. You will see in these pages. I get a big article written about me in the New York Daily Newspaper and John Lennon gets shot the day before it's published, so the entire article gets preempted in all the NY city editions. (It was picked up on UPI and ran in the strangest places all over the country, though, like Boca Raton.) Then 3 years later, we get a cover story in the Sunday Daily News, with color pictures of me, and a snow storm prevents delivery in the New York area. I can't make this stuff up. It happens over and over. I didn't make the party, had to settle for the Ice cream.

While we were still poor, we were not the poorest, not even close. My father worked for the city. He also had a part time job as a bouncer at a restaurant. And, one as a pin boy at a bowling alley. The alley and the restaurant, Emil's, were both in a building on Park Row in NYC.

Sometimes, on holidays, dad would take us to the bowling alley and open it up for us. Few people know that in the old days, the pins sat on spikes and as soon as they were set, a pin boy dropped the spikes and the pins stayed still until they were knocked down by the balls. The pin boy picked up the balls too. Going to the alley was fun but it was a lot of work too, so I don't think we ever got a full game in.

Dad also was a member of the American Legion, with a weekly meeting, and he went to see his mother on Wednesday nights, and he worked two nights a week at the bar. So I really was raised exclusively by my mother, who drank a lot. Maybe because my father was never around.

Both my parents were pretty smart. My mother was smarter than my father. But she never went to school. Almost literally, she went as far as the 8th grade only. Her life gave meaning to the old movies where the girls would only go to grammar school and then cry because they had to then go to work. She was bitter about the fact that her brothers all went to high school and she was ashamed about her own lack of education.

By the time I was in school, all the girls went to high school because that was the law. Lots of kids dropped out at 16, and no one cried over not being able to go to school. But the way my mother told it, had she gone to high school, who knows how successful she would have been? No doubt she would have avoided marrying my father, her ultimate ruination, to hear her tell it. My father was, in terms of the 20s and 30s, rather well educated. He finished high school and even had a little college. He worked for the city. My mother said he had no ambition. He said he wanted the security of a government job. Of course, nowadays, government jobs have no security anymore, but then, they pay better now, relatively speaking, than they did back then. But they never ever got fired. Civil servants now are solid middle class; we were not - we were low class.

I was thinking about this the other day. I had a plastic coat. It was really plastic. We called them leather jackets - I guess they were vinyl. They would tear like a piece of paper. But mostly everyone had these leather coats. That was back in Brooklyn. I skated on the street in the kind of skates that you needed a key for. You put them over your shoes and tightened the grip with a key. I had the cheap ones. The grip was only the sides of the shoe, not over the foot like the more expensive ones. I was a really good skater, but the fact that the macadam in Brooklyn was extremely smooth helped. When I moved to Queens I stopped skating.

Hormones start kicking in, too. The bottom line was that I was chubby from 10 to 12. That wasn't the worst experience with moving. I went from a school that loved me to a school that, well, didn't love me. I was a mutt, half Irish and half Syrian. My neighborhood in Brooklyn was very mixed, with a lot of Irish and Scandinavians. When I moved, at 9, I landed in a 95% Italian neighborhood. Also, you had to pay for the school, about $50/month, whereas the one in Brooklyn was free. Did I mention we were talking catholic schools here?

The teachers picked on me because my mother didn't always pay on time. It was very cliquish. The other parents were quite involved with the school and the church, which was smallish, not like the almost Cathedral we had at Our Lady of Angels. So I had friends, and did extremely well, but I was always on the outside with the nuns. When I graduated, I had the highest average in the grade, 98.1. But I got an S in conduct. That S, I am told, prevented me from getting the academic award at graduation. They did give me a medal for Math though. My average in Math was 100.

Catholic schools have an indelible effect on the kids that go there. Nowadays that may be somewhat positive, I can't say. As for back then, it was not. Most girls remember dress and behavior rules, like not wearing patent letter shoes. Boys remember the spankings and the knuckles, and horribly sometimes, the priests. A lot of the discipline related to suppressing sexuality especially in the higher grades. I remember parent's day in my 8th grade. I was thinking, as usual, I would get glowing remarks and my parents would come home proud. I can still picture what happened. My mother flew into the house in a rage. She started slapping me and hitting me. I went down in a crouch while she continued to batter. I was 13 and almost full size so I wasn't getting hurt so much, but I was shaken, and incredulous. When she finally calmed down I learned what happened.

First the teacher told my mother that I was an excellent student. But - big but, she said I was "frustrated". That was a word with a hell of a lot of weight in 1962. The nun told my mother that I slouched in my chair and opened and closed my legs. This was tantamount to telling my mother I was a sexual deviate. I don't really know why the teacher would have done this, but my mother was crazed. I ultimately convinced my mother that I was innocent and she let up. From then on, she hated this one nun. I had hated her long before.

This nun, Sr. Patricia, also picked on my hair. I finally cut it all off and then she told my mother I didn't have to cut it, it looked nice one day. All catholic school kid's journals are filled with stuff like this.

The big thing about Catholicism for me was the sexism. It was subtle and devastating. Here is how it worked. Students all knew the pecking order. The teachers were to be treated with the utmost of respect. It was all nuns back then. Then there was mother superior. If she was spotted, you went the other way. Nuns feared and deferred to her. But still, she was another mortal. But a priest - A priest was special; a priest was a god. If priests were going to come into the classroom, special preparations were made. We were taught how to speak and not speak to them. Obviously, any girl or boy, for that matter, would notice that all nuns were women and priests were men. So the people of authority that came into our school lives established the superiority of men. This was true in our home lives too. Mothers stayed home, fathers went out to work. Doctors, the true gods of society, were almost always men. So, too, for policemen, firemen. Television reinforced the stereotype. If you were a girl, you might have been told you could be anything you wanted, that was part of the post war change that came to my generation. No one believed it, but they said it. But no matter how strong, how smart, how hardworking – a girl could NEVER be a priest. And to me that meant that the lowest performing boy in the class was better than me. It meant that to all the boys too. They may have feared the nuns but they all knew some day they, by virtue of their gender, would be superior to the nuns too.

This "knowing" is a pervasive sore that eats away at a child's psyche. In me, it planted the seeds of a rage that would not come to full bloom until I was in my 40's. Growing up in a catholic school classroom, even today, carries a message of gender inequality. Catholicism today is still about gender inequality, and male domination. Women will never be priests in the Catholic Church.

I went to catholic school and the logical step was then to go to Catholic High School. There was something called Diocesan schools which were relatively cheap and supposedly good. I wanted to go to Bronx High School of Science but that was way too far away. Brooklyn Tech and Stuyvesant didn't accept girls back then, so I couldn't go to those much closer schools even if my mother let me. But my mother would not have allowed it, there was no Saint in the name. The nuns at school also never mentioned a word about Bronx Science or Hunter High School, although several of our boys who were not nearly as good at Math as I was were sent to Brooklyn Tech.

So I went to a Diocesan school called Christ the King which had just opened only the year before. It was called a co-educational school but the only thing co-ed about it was that boys and girls were schooled in the same building. We did not share classes or eat together.

Christ the King did something which I have always abhorred and truly believe is counterproductive and ineffective. They divided each class into three groups. There were the average students in several sections and then there were one or two sections for the high achievers, and one for those who needed special help. I have always felt that students learn from other students, and unless you are talking about advanced classes, they should be intermingled. Certainly there is no reason whatsoever to separate them into sections and label them.

I was in the high performing group. I was doing very well, except sometimes I got something called signatures for talking in the hall or the like. You carried a card with you and if a nun saw you doing something you weren't supposed to do, they would sign your card. Enough signatures and you got detention or worse. But other than for signatures, I did OK, except for one big thing.

People always thought I was tough, or worse, that *I* thought I was tough. There were two tough girls in the "smart class". You could tell by their hair. Teased hair was a big thing in 1963 and they had teased hair. And they might have smoked. Well, neither of these girls liked me for some reason, maybe because they were really tough and people thought I was tough and they did not like that.

I took two buses to get to school. You could also take three trains, but obviously the buses made more sense. A lot of the girls in the bottom class took my bus. Some of them were a bit radical, like they rolled up their uniform skirts and changed their shoes after they got out of the sight of the school. But the worst ever, is that some dabbled in smoking. Cigarettes. This was long before pot hit. So these troublesome girls, who were really just like all the other girls except they were pre-determined to get in trouble because they were in the bottom group, and everyone loves a self-fulfilling prophesy, could be seen smoking cigarettes on the back of the bus, my bus, and someone ratted them out. I am pretty it was one of the "high performing" but tough girls.

This one low group girl who lived real close to me, Theresa, but wasn't from my grammar school, which would have created a relationship between us, got nailed for smoking. That was big time. Her parents were brought in, and she got all sorts of heavy duty detentions, and probably got the shit kicked out of her from her low performing old man, no doubt. Guess who got blamed for telling? Me! I was fingered as the rat.

Now, as I live and breathe, I have never been a rat. But even if I was, truth be told, I was scared shitless by this girl, and her other low performing friends. They were like a gang to me. I acted fearless but I was not. I knew Theresa smoked but that is a fact that would have gone to my grave, believe me.

Theresa decided she needed to get me. Within one day, the word was all over the school. They were going to wait for Friday, two days later, and then they were going to get me and beat me up. I have been lucky in life in that I have never confronted real danger. The closest I ever got was almost drowning and I was too busy staying alive to feel the taste of fear. When Theresa's gang mobilized to get me, it was as if I was facing a pack of wolves. I will never forget the terror I experienced for the longest hour of my life, the day they came after me.

The school bell rang and it was time to go home. I thought I would just wait it out. I would hide in school until they went home. But they weren't going. Buses came and left and the girls were waiting there. I decided to take the train. The way to the station was sort of round about and I got there without being seen. As I stepped onto the train, I saw on the station that several of Theresa's "girls" were there as well. Someone saw me. This was a terminal station so the train sat for several minutes. As they mounted the train, I ran through the cars desperate. I spotted a girl I knew and asked her to hide me. I got on the floor and she threw a coat over me and put her book bag on top. We saw the girls pass through the car and get off again. Then the train started moving.

This girl I was with was in one or two of my classes, or maybe she was in my section. I know I did not know her too well but she was in the high group. I had no idea where she lived. It was Bushwick. I went home with her and called my parents from her house. My father came and got me. I never saw her again.

This incident had happened around the holidays, right before the beginning of the new term. My parents called the school and we had a meeting with the Mother Superior or the Dean of Girls. I explained everything that happened and they told me Theresa would be expelled. I didn't want her expelled, I just wanted to get the hell away. Nothing my parents or the dean (who wanted to keep me there) could say would convince me to stay at that school. I was finished. Even if Theresa was not there, the other girls would be. I was afraid they would kill me, especially since she was being thrown out. I was irrational. I told my mother to enroll me in the public high school where my sister and brother had gone and that was it. That was the end of catholic education for me. So I went to John Adams High School in Ozone Park which I could walk to. I was enrolled in section A41 and put into all the same classes I was taking at Christ the King, including biology, which is a sophomore level class at Adams but I had started it already, so they had me continue. I never got to take earth science which is what the freshmen take at Adams, so I don't know anything about rocks.

It is not easy to start in a new school in the middle of the year, when everyone is already settled in. Especially when you're a freshman and especially when there are 4000 students and a massive building with byzantine hallways and stairs. I did as well as I could. I got through lunch and the first period after lunch and went into my freshman history class. Who walks in? It's Theresa. I thought I would have a heart attack. She didn't say a word. I was afraid to even look at her. She sat right next to me.

I was afraid to tell my parents because I thought they might go up to Adams and make trouble. My brother was still there - he was a senior. Even though that gave me a level of comfort, and he walked me to and from school, I still feared going to class every day for about two weeks. Then a miracle happened. We had a test. Theresa looked at me and I immediately knew the score. I took my paper and moved it over to her side of the desk. If it was any closer to her, it would have been in her lap. We did that test together. She never bothered me for help again. She never bothered me period. I suppose she knew it was the end of the line for her, too, but she kept up the intimidation, and I capitulated. I only looked tough. She was the real thing.

I often think about her. I don't even remember what happened to her in school, I never followed up on what she was doing, and I was no longer afraid of her. I think we might have said hi to each other in the hallways, but we probably never had a conversation. I hope she is doing well. My gut tells me that getting her out of Christ the King might have been the best thing for her, not being pigeon-holed into the low group.

High school was a romp for me. I just did great. We didn't have homogenous groups but we did have two sections that were called honors sections. There were no slow sections. The kids in honors took mostly honors classes, although anyone who excelled in a subject could take an honors class, if they could handle the work. Sort of the same thing as AP classes which were just starting out when I was in school. The only thing that wasn't honors was chemistry and physics. I guess they figured those subjects were hard enough as it was. In sophomore year, I met Mrs. Troyano. She taught Geometry. I did extremely well in her class, and I got a 98 in the first semester. New York was a Regents state which meant that at the end of the year, you had to take a state wide exam. Geometry was a subject that had a Regents. I had gotten 100 on every test and I asked Mrs. T if she would give me a 100 for a final grade. She said no. I said what the hell, of course not in those words and she told me no teacher would ever give a student 100 in any subject. I said that is totally wrong and unfair and she said no one is perfect and 100 means perfection, to which I replied I had a perfect record in her class. She used to give these one example quizzes all the time, what she called extra 10's and if you got it you got extra credit and if you didn't, it wouldn't count. Of course, I also got all the extra 10's, too.

I need to interject here. Likely you have already concluded I am no genius. I agree. But I have a natural talent for Math like some people have natural talents for art and music. I basically owned any math I saw, at least until college. I loved Geometry. I would do examples for fun. I did all my math homework because I did it so easily. A doctor friend of mine recently reminded me that I got him through the Geometry Regents which I had totally forgotten because I loved Geometry and now I recall getting every one of my friends a good grade on that test. Anyway, Mrs. Troyano made a deal with me. She said if I got 100 on the Regents she would give me 100 as a final grade. So I did, and she was true to her word, and I have the Report Card to prove it. My three math state wides were 99, 100 and 98 - Algebra, Geometry and Trigonometry. I won the school's two year math medal! Adams had one guidance counselor in a high school of 4000, and she met with me once. Her guidance was for me to become a math teacher. I suppose she never heard of engineering or research. Teach! I admire teachers but I was engineering material, MIT material, as a matter of fact. I was a girl. I am not even sure if MIT took girls then. I know neither Columbia nor Harvard were taking girls. I was steered to Queens College because I had a high average and Queens was very competitive. I knew about CCNY's reputation and I decided to apply there. Back in those days it was said that girls only went to college to get an MRS. But that's not entirely true, some went to become teachers. Nursing was not even a baccalaureate degree then.

Mrs. Troyano had once told me to go to Cornell. But that was when I was a sophomore. Her daughter was in Ithaca College and she was certain I could get into Cornell. But she retired from teaching after my sophomore year and I forgot that idea because I didn't even know where it was. Turns out Cornell was always co-educational, and this was her way of trying to send me to an Ivy League school.

I started doing a lot of what they call service in sophomore year. I did everything from handing out programs at the school events to making copies for teachers. There weren't many copier machines. We used something called a mimeograph which you had to crank and you could get purple ink on you. Plus the copies ran, so you could blur the ink if you were not careful.

I got a really important job over the winter vacation. (What kind of idiot goes into school during the winter vacation?) I worked in the Dean of Girl's office and I worked very hard. Over time, the Dean got used to seeing me around and she had me do some things for her directly. Finally, she just co-opted me and made me her personal assistant. Mrs. Kean, the dean, loved me.

There was this thing called Girl's State. It was run by the American Legion. They still have it now but it is very different. At the time, they took only one girl from each school in the state and sent them to Albany for a week to study government. They had one for boys too. Bill Clinton made this program famous because he went on to Boy's Nation, where that ubiquitous picture of him and John Kennedy comes from. The honors section teachers were asked to nominate a few students. My teacher did not nominate me. Actually, she didn't like me too much. Maybe because I talked in class so much. My overall experience with teachers is that they either got me or they didn't get me. And sometimes when they didn't get me, they didn't like me. I could be what looked like disrespectful to someone who didn't know me well. I had a mouth. Mrs. Bell didn't know me for shit, and she liked me even less.

When the Dean saw the girl's names come in and mine wasn't on it, she just trashed the list and picked me herself. Right after the semester ended, off I went to Girl's State.

This was the first time I had ever been away from home. I roomed in a dorm at Albany State College, which was brand new, with two other girls. It was like heaven to me. We went to class every day, ate relatively good food, and spent our evenings together hanging out in this massive lounge that had vending machines where we could dance and drink cokes and smoke if we were so inclined. I made friends with everyone. Back then I was less shy than I am now, very outgoing. They divided us into two groups that they called parties. The Nationalists and the Federalists. I was a Federalist. First we learned about the branches of government and political parties. The plan was for us to learn all about caucusing and putting together a platform and then each side would run its own candidates for office and we would have an election. I wrote our party's campaign theme song. It was called "When you're a Fed" after the song "When you're a Jet" from West Side Story. I sang it at the rally. The one line I remember is "little Nats step aside or we'll use pesticide."

When the time came to pick candidates, I was chosen to run for Governor. I wanted to run for Comptroller though because my father worked in the Comptroller's office in NY and I thought he would like that, so I ran for Comptroller. Pretty stupid, huh? Our advisors told us that when we voted, we were to pick the best candidate, not vote along party lines. The Nationalist's advisors told them party first, just vote for the platform period. Sort of like Democrats and Republicans today. Anyway, the Nationalists won in a clean sweep with a landslide for the entire ticket. I wonder if that was planned. There certainly is a lesson in it. Since I was nominated for something, I ended up being designated Minority Leader of the Assembly.

At the end of the week, all the girls got together and selected one girl to go to Girl's Nation in Washington D.C., the national equivalent of Girl's State. I was picked!

In what I recall as one of the stupidest mistakes of my life, I didn't go. I was trying to get a summer job with the City of NY where my father worked, and we felt that if I missed the first week of the job to go to Washington, I might lose it altogether. Imagine. So I didn't go to Girl's nation. Where the hell were my parent's brains? I'll tell you where. Concerned about the chance for me to make a total of $400 working that summer. We weren't stupid, we were poor and we thought like poor people do. That I still regret this after 45 years is kind of scary, no?

I had already been interested in politics when I was in high school. I was recruited to run for class representative in sophomore year. They asked kids in the honors sections to do this. Makes a lot of sense right? Just keep going to the haves. Anyway I agreed to run and I was up against this nice girl Linda. She was so nice I even voted for her. I think it was part of my catholic upbringing - the sin of pride. Anyway, I lost. But I ran the next semester and I won and I ran and won the following year and then when I was a senior I won Vice President of the School. (Boys are presidents - not girls).

I would have gotten into a bit of trouble in high school if I had not been an honor student. For instance, I got nailed smoking and got away with it. One thing I did was really bad. I was taking chemistry at the time and had just learned about nitrous oxide which is a yellow gas that is produced when nitric acid comes into contact with certain metals. They used to use it to test for gold because the acid does not react with gold. We had done an experiment in class with some metal, maybe tin or lead, who knows, and produced a yellowish gas which everyone thought was cool. My best friend, Lydia, and I had spotted a bracelet in a drawer in one of the tables of the chem lab and decided we should test if it was gold. So, after school was out, we snuck into the chem lab, which was pretty easy to do in those days. We filled a beaker with nitric acid and dropped the bracelet in it. It was like a bomb went off. The lab and then the whole hallway filled with yellow gas. Our teacher, Miss Keneally came running out of her classroom which was near the lab. She did something to get it under control. We were freaked out. There weren't many people around and she covered for us. I should have gotten suspended. Keneally was pissed because it was her bracelet. Plus we did a fucking stupid dangerous thing. But secretly, I know she loved the idea that we went back, on our own, after school, to do an experiment. Miss Keneally was the quintessential teacher. She won a major national award in her later years recognizing that fact. I got to write a recommendation for her. Miss Keneally really liked me. So much so that my mother was convinced she was a lesbian, god forbid, and wanted me to stay away from her. I know that she loved my intelligence and interest in learning and she nurtured me as she had done with other students before and after. First she started buying me things. Like once she heard us singing the "Feeling Groovy" song and she bought me the Simon and Garfunkel album with that on it. She bought me unusual things, like when I started dying my hair she bought me hair dye and conditioner because she didn't want me putting any cheap crap into my hair. She gave me tickets to a play and to the opera. But the big thing was, when I wanted to learn to drive, she gave me driving lessons and she got me lessons from an expert as well.

The kids in school thought she was cool because she drove a 1966 Chevy Impala 327 with a stick shift. It was a hot car. So I learned to drive in a hot rod with a stick. Keneally gave me more than gifts though. Miss Keneally was one of the most important, and maybe the single most influential person in my life. She saw what I had beyond the very rough edges. Mrs. Troyano did and so did Mrs. Kean, but Miss Keneally dedicated herself to my success. I was good in Chemistry but I was not the best. I didn't like Chemistry theory but what I did like was balancing equations. The Math part. Miss Keneally gave me equations to balance from a college textbook and gave me and anyone else who could do it extra credit. That's what got me up to a 92 in Chemistry, no way the highest mark, but nothing to be ashamed about. She remained my friend until the too early end of her life. I could and did discuss everything with her. We met up every so many years and had lunch or dinner. Once, I took her through Trump Tower and introduced her to Donald. I introduced them to each other as the two greatest influences of my life. It was half true, anyway.

Most unfortunately, Mrs. Kean retired after my Junior Year. With Mrs. Troyano gone, that was the end of my major champions in High School, and there were plenty of detractors. On the student council, I was openly critical of things like the cafeteria and the newspaper and red card policies and the new people on the staff were not crazy about my bluntness. I made teacher enemies and I had no rabbi left.

This was the first year for a new principal and he did not know the ropes or who was who. Somehow he got the idea that I was a troublemaker and blamed me for something bad that happened, which, for the life of me, I cannot remember. All I know is I didn't do it, but I was accused and then exonerated and he actually apologized to me. But like I said, I had no supporters left except Ms. Keneally and she did not have the kind of juice that others had, she couldn't do much for me outside of her own classroom. So when graduation came, I got the distinguished service award, because I had more than the necessary service credits, but that was it. A few days after graduation, I got an award from the American Society of Math teachers for excellence in Mathematics in the mail.

I don't regret a day of my high school life. I was not one of the "popular" kids because that was a very special clique to which I could not belong. But the school politics made me popular and I also sang in a few shows. One time, my two friends played guitar and we sang two songs together and then I sang "The House of the Rising Sun" by myself. The other time, it was the senior night, I got dressed up in a gown I borrowed from my friend, Jeanne's mother and I sang "Summer Time" with a jazz band. Most of the 4000 kids knew my name and I liked being famous to them. For the yearbook the seniors vote their "bests". I was named, "Done most for Adams" and I thought that was a nice honor, screw the new administration.

During the summer between high school and college I worked for the City of New York in another position my father was able to finagle for me. It was with the Department of Welfare. My job was to go through applications made by doctors for coverage under Medicaid. I was able to tell right then and there that people were gaming the system. It's hysterical. It took the bureaucracy a long time to come up with the scofflaws but a lot of doctors were prosecuted for cheating on Medicaid. Some doctors had like $500,000 in payable bills. It just didn't make sense. But I had no one I could tell and if I spotted it so easily, I am sure that many others had to and realized there was fraud involved. Most likely their work led to the investigation which exposed and convicted many crook doctors. It was an interesting point in an otherwise extremely boring job. The good part was the mayor had a program for poor kids which gave them jobs for the city and Welfare got three kids. I became friends with them, but by comparison, I lived like a millionaire. These kids came from tough places and hard lives. But when you're 17, you can find fun in unusual places, and we did. I learned a lot that summer.

I was planning to enter college in September 1967 as a computer science major. I had come across a program that was training students in a work/study program at Pace University and I wanted to enroll in that, but I was talked out of it, mainly by my sister, because Pace did not have anything like the reputation or name recognition of CCNY. I often wonder what would have happened to me if I had been on the ground floor in the computer industry. Anyway, I kept the idea in my mind, but that was only a dalliance. I knew what I wanted to be. So I entered the class of 1971 as a pre-law student.

Chapter 2 - Becoming an Engineer

    For my first semester courses, I signed up for Political Science, French, Calculus (go figure), History, Music and Gym. I didn't know anyone at the school except a boy from my Physics class in High School. He was two years older than me and an engineering student. We had gone out for a while before my mother put a stop to it. (He was Chinese). Anyway, he introduced me to all his friends and I started hanging out with the engineering kids who convinced me to change my major to engineering. So by the end of the first year, I was going for an engineering degree. Since I had not taken surveying, I would be behind my class if I chose Mechanical or Civil, and I sucked at Chemistry (except for balancing equations) so I went with Electrical, which would be best for me anyway, because it was all Math. And that is the story of how I became an electrical engineer. (Plus I always liked circuits in high school Physics)

    I didn't encounter a lot of sexism in the beginning. At least that I know of. But later, when I took a particularly hard course in Power Engineering, (it was about motors and lots of Math), and I did OK, that is to say, I got a C. The way we got our grades was you gave the teacher a postcard when you took the final exam, and the grade would be mailed to you. But the grades themselves were also posted on a list on the classroom door. Most of us went to look for the grades. I was coming around the corner of the hallway heading toward that subject's door and there was a group of students standing outside looking over the grades. I heard one of them say, "she must have slept with him (meaning the teacher) for that grade". There were no A's and maybe a few B's and there were a few F's too. This would not be the only time I was accused of fooling around with the teacher to get a grade. Or fooling around with the boss, for that matter. But it was a rude awakening to me. How could anyone have thought that? First off, I was a virgin, not that this was anyone's business. Secondly, the teacher was about 60. Did the kids really think I slept with him? No, I am sure they didn't. It was the fact that they said it. They spoke about me that way, so disrespectfully. Also, they made it obvious that they didn't think I, a girl, was smart enough to pass this class, much less get a C! This experience changed the way I looked at my fellow students. There was no question of the animus, and I would separate the friends from the foes, from that day on.

I had trouble in classes with teachers too. I will never forget, Control Systems, with Vincent Del Toro, who used his own book. He had two classes. I was in the first one. When he walked into the other class he said, "Thank god there are no girls in this class. I hate teaching girls." And he showed it too. He gave me a D. No way did I deserve a D, but I could tell the way he treated me in class that I was not going to get a decent grade from this guy.

Strangely, I also had a problem with a female teacher. Engineers took a class called Humanities. It was only for engineers and was

Literature, Philosophy, Art History, and the like rolled into one. The teacher was not accustomed to having girls in her class. She used to sit on the desk, in her straight skirt, with her legs crossed. She was probably about 35 and liked being around the boys. She didn't like sharing the spotlight. (Am I being sexist here? Probably not because this is what I thought, as a kid in the class, and she made me feel very self-conscious with her antics.)

We were reading Lysistrata in the class. For the uninformed, Lysistrata is a Greek Comedy wherein the women of the community manifest their dissatisfaction with the activities of their husbands as a group, by going on a sex strike. It is surprisingly graphic. The teacher decided we should read it aloud in class and she gave me a part to read. Of course, I had not prepared by reading the play in the homework assignment so I didn't know what was coming and as I read, I realized I was describing a woman's pubic hair. I was so humiliated that I put the book down, said, "I am not reading this shit," and walked out of the classroom.

Women can harass other women and this is what happened. She was in a position of superiority, had control of me, and used sex to exercise that control. I was not the hardened "fuck you too", construction worker that I eventually grew into, and this really hurt me. She put me in my place, had all the boys laugh at me, and goaded me into actions that could jeopardize my grade. I did not like this woman.

Engineering has a lot of labs and they were maintained by technicians from the local neighborhood which was Harlem. The techs all liked me. At the time there was a very vocal Congresswomen from NY named Bella Abzug, who was famous for her mouth, her hats and her position on civil rights and women's rights too. She became one of my personal heroes. Bella was on in years and she was not attractive. But she did a lot for New York and all the people in Harlem liked her, including the lab technicians. Because they perceived me as a woman's rights fighter, they gave me a nickname - "the beautiful Bella" and that is how I was known to them. The fact that they called me beautiful was not sexist, because they did not intend it that way, nor did they call me that in front of students. It wasn't until later that I realized the techs related to me. There were very few black students in City College back then, I don't recall any engineers, although there may have been a few. Remember, the bulk of the students in engineering were Jewish and Italian. So I think they bonded with me because I was the only female, and they understood the challenges faced by "the other" in an empathetic way.

While I was taking labs, something important was going on in connection with women's rights, which I was always sprouting at school. In 1971, it was legal for a public place to just ban women. Very much the same as it had been, less than 10 years earlier, when some restaurants in the United States just banned black people. There was a very famous bar called McSorley's in the village that didn't allow women patrons. No ladies. I knew of this place years earlier because my sister went to night school at Cooper Union, in the same neighborhood. The guys would go for a beer after school and my sister was left out. Learning this really affected me. I was only 11, but I understood all the nuances. Elaine was made to feel unequal and she was forced to miss out on the camaraderie of socializing with her classmates. It angered me even more than her, I think. In fact, women were barred from hundreds of restaurants, clubs and bars. Even the politicians held an annual dinner with no women, so the Mayor and the Governor were there, but Bella couldn't go.

This year, when I was the beautiful Bella, there was a federal discrimination lawsuit against McSorley's and it was big news. The women won. The lab technicians understood the meaning of the victory and subsequent legislation forcing McSorley's to serve women and making it against the law to discriminate against women in a public place. They had been there. They were great guys and I enjoyed chatting with them and hanging out. Besides, the labs were so damned boring, I spent half the time talking to them. I liked talking civil rights and women's' rights and they were better listeners than my fellow students.

I took a job at Macy's, in December 1967, for the Christmas crunch. I got laid off after New Year's but they called me back to work permanently and my hours were 5:30 to 9:30 on

Tuesdays and Wednesdays, and 12:30 to 9:30 on Saturday. That was 16 hours per week. My regent's scholarship paid for my books and registration fee. (CCNY was free so I got cash for my scholarship.) My mother gave me $10 a week for transportation and lunch and the Macy's money was for spending. I did a lot with that $24 a week. I really liked working at Macy's, especially when it was busy. My friend Pat and I were like a team, I did the register and she did the wrapping. We would go to other parts of the store to find big lines and then we would ask if we could go help out. Pat and I cleaned up a line in a few minutes. Everything was manual. A sales clerk got 2 weeks of training on the register, but most of them were pretty slow. First there were no credit cards, then later we got machines that you physically typed the number into. Anyway, working fast like that was fun. Of course when it was slow I was constantly getting chewed out for leaving the floor or talking. We were supposed to move the stock around and look busy when we had free time.

As an employee of Macy's, I was able to participate in the parade. We had a choice of being a character or holding a balloon which paid 50% more. (That's $9, instead of $6) I did not weigh enough to hold a balloon. One year, I was an "Indian" paddling a canoe with my friend while we were chased by cowboys on horses. Of course the canoes and horses were props. But of all things to put on the front page of the Times the next day, don't you know there was an overhead shot of our ridiculous carryings on. The other year, I was a Santa's Helper, so I got to wear a tiny red skirt and a white sweater and freeze my ass off for 2 hours walking next to The Big Guy and waving at the little kids. It was an amazing experience because the kids all thought this was the real Santa and they stared at him with pure adulation. Made you believe in Christmas.

Being at the parade, by itself, was a magical experience. I saw the Mummers who were grown men dressed in fantastic feather costumes who danced and played music. There were marching bands from everywhere, and they were great. There were crazy floats with TV and Movie stars on them. Then, there were the balloons, which I was amazed to see were so enormous in person. I was like a child myself. My heart soared with Bullwinkle and The Underdog. Everyone should go to the parade in person at least once in their lives.

The year I was Santa's Helper, I was taking Mechanical Drawing, a fancy name for drafting. It was a goddam two credit course that had so much homework, but I was fortunate to find someone willing to do mine for me. (This kid liked me and drove me home from school. There were lots of boys like that, and I suppose I took advantage, but I never went out with any of them.) I did draw some basic machines, and also I had excellent printing which probably accounts for my getting a C, but the teacher liked me, too. He talked to me a lot and learned about my upcoming Parade appearance and told me he would try to make it. Not knowing how fantastic the parade was, I said to myself, "why?" Anyway with a million people there, I figured I would never see him. Damned if he wasn't there with his little boy. He found me and introduced me to his son. At the time I was kind of creeped out, but now I realize that he was being friendly and really was nice to me and was never out of line. And of course, I was happy to take the grade. Again, it was said I slept with the teacher.

In the summers, I lied to get work. Back then, there were no summer jobs, or let me say no jobs for my class of people. My father could not pull off a hat trick, so for my third summer of working age, I had to apply for permanent positions saying I quit school. This was not particularly honorable, but on the other hand, anyone I worked for got their money's worth out of me. The first job I got was with a reinsurance company. I told them I went to school for a year and decided to drop out. I worked all summer and when I quit at the end of August, they told me they expected it, but they were very nice about it. Next year I went to work as a statistical typist. I knew I was only going to keep that job for 6 weeks because I was going to Europe. That was the worst god forsaken job, typing numbers on ledgers. Both summers I continued to work at Macy's so I was working 6 days and two nights a week. For my summer between junior and senior years I just worked at Macy's and went to the beach during the day.

I was sexually harassed twice at work that I can remember. The first was at the reinsurance company. There was this guy that would keep giving me stuff to copy. When I brought the copies into his office he would detain me. He kept asking me about my boyfriend and telling me how pretty I was and any boy would be lucky to have me. This made me terribly uncomfortable. He used to sit in his chair at the edge of the desk so I could see his body. He would put his leg up on something, maybe a box, that was near his seat and he would shake his leg. I could see he had an erection but at the time, I did not know exactly what that meant, just that it was disgusting. He had pictures of his little kids in the office. I tried to stay away from him but he did this to me at least a half a dozen times. Of course I did not report it. Imagine reporting something like that in 1968?

The other time was at Macy's. There was this guy who was a manager in the men's department but we all knew him and he was very nice, albeit a bit creepy. He worked the night shift and was a graduate student in the daytime studying Psychology, or so he said. He asked me if I would be part of a study. He cleared it with my manager and took me into the back office and asked me a series of mostly innocuous questions which I answered. Then he asked me to stand up. He said to imagine I had just taken a shower, and I walked out naked and someone was standing there, what would I do with my hands, would I cover my breasts or my genital area. I remember telling him I would try to cover both and then said I had to go back to work. I should have socked him in the nose. Later, I spoke to some girls in the other departments that I knew from around and they said he did the same thing to them. No one reported it. We just took it and were a little wiser for the experience. I think if we had gotten together and reported it, the guy would have lost his job. But you didn't think that way, back then. He was a manager and we were sales girls.

In the summer between my two senior years in college, that is the fourth and fifth years because engineering was five years, I decided to try to get a job in a related field. My sister worked for Diesel Construction Company in New York as an executive secretary. Actually, she had the knowledge and intelligence to be the company president, or at least, a project manager. She was just a few years too early. (It turns out she was way way too early. Project managers with the exception of anomalies like me didn't really show up in the construction industry until the 1990s.) Anyway, she got me a job at a company called Zwicker Electric Company. Zwicker was an electrical subcontractor that installed electric work in commercial and residential buildings. They did a lot of work for Diesel which was one of the main General Contractors in New York and my sister's employers. Zwicker hired me as a favor to Elaine, and, of course, her boss. Elaine had tremendous power because she controlled all access to the president of the company. She also processed work orders and extras and could stop a job or a subcontractor cold. Of course, she was also extremely well liked for her intelligence and personality so it was easy to do her a favor.

I reported to Zwicker on a June morning in 1971 wearing a miniskirt. The job was going to be drafting. I took drafting in college because it was a requirement for engineers. Actually, we called it mechanical drawing. That was the course with the teacher who went to see me in the Macy's parade. At the very least, I was qualified to work a part time summer job for an electrical contractor with 4 years of engineering school, and mechanical drawing under my belt.

I was assigned to work for a man named Al Silverman who was the assistant project manager on the Mount Sinai Hospital and School of Medicine Building that was under construction in New York. He started me on something called slab drawings, which I will explain later. Unfortunately, the drafting department did not have desks, it had drafting tables, and I was given one to sit at. Needless to say, I sat at a stool, which is not something you would sit at wearing a skirt unless there was a bar in front of it. I was sitting there with the world open to my legs for about an hour, and then the man (kid) I was working directly opposite to came over and taped a large drawing to the front of my desk as a sort of vanity panel.

Slabs are the concrete floors that you see in most buildings. The way some concrete floors are made is they are first framed out in plywood. Then reinforcing bars are installed over the wood and concrete is poured over them. When the concrete is properly cured, the wood is stripped and voila! You have a slab. In a commercial building, the slab is usually thick enough to accommodate pipe through which the wires are pulled to connect the lights, and motors and circuits. The pipe goes on to the reinforcing bars before the slab is poured. Also anything passing through a slab must have a sleeve installed before the concrete is poured so you don't have to chop the concrete later to get it through. That would jeopardize the structural integrity of the slab. Same thing is done with a box for pipe shafts. Lots of preparations need to be made before the floor is actually poured.

In a hospital there is a whole lot of electric; everything is connected to something else. Therefore, there is a massive amount of wiring, and as much as possible goes into the slab for several reasons. First it is cheaper. Conduit just lays on the rebar and it goes in easy - very labor friendly. Secondly, it is most efficient for the building because the ceiling spaces are filled with ductwork and lighting and large pipes that cannot fit into the slab, like heating and plumbing. Small electric just gets in the way so everyone wants as much electrical conduit in the slab as possible.

I had taken an electrical wiring course in college so I could basically read the drawings. Basically is an understatement because contract drawings are extremely difficult to read. There are symbols for every kind of device and there is a symbol list. Lines are drawn connecting symbol to symbol and the lines are labeled with the number of wires and the size of pipe, e.g. 4 #12, ¾" gal, which tells you that there will be a ¾" inside diameter galvanized pipe and four wires will be pulled through it. Well, anyway, I had to lay out all the pipe on a plan so that a layout man could put the empty conduit on the rebars, and after the slab was poured and hardened, the electricians would later pull the wires through the conduit now buried in the slab. I had to determine the location where the conduit turned up and down and designate it on the plan so the layout man knew where to stop the pipe and put an elbow. This would happen where there was a wall or a box in the floor or something in the space below the slab.

Therefore, I needed to learn how to read the architectural drawings as well so I could dimension the ups and downs which were marked with X's and O's just like hugs and kisses. The paper (actually I worked on mylar which is like a plastic that you can draw on with a pencil) was enormous, much bigger than a regular plan.

I loved doing this work and I was really good at it. I did the 7th and 8th floors where there were operating rooms and intensive care units. They were pouring the slabs on a very fast cycle so the need for the drawings was acute. I was asked to work overtime which I did. I even brought a plan home with me to work on at my dining room table. There wasn't enough light in my house to see the yellow highlighter I had to use on the plans, so I went out and bought a 300W light bulb. Lucky I didn't burn the house down. Smart about plans, stupid about house wiring.

Toward the end of the summer, my boss Al decided to take me and some of the full time guys up to the job site to see our work. This meant walking the deck which means walking on the plywood and stepping around the reinforcing bars.

Ever since the second day of work, I was wearing pants to the office and my shoes were the kind of shoes in style then, which were like a combination of sneakers and work boots, so I was good to go for the field. And, I was extremely excited to do this.

We had lunch in a surprisingly nice place, and then went to the hospital. I had never been to a construction site, and I suppose I might have stood out, but I am not sure why. From a distance, you would not be able to tell whether I was a girl or a boy (of course, up close, this was not the case.) Anyway, we went to the field office, donned hard hats and went up to the floor on the construction elevator. And it was fun. I saw the pipes that I had placed on the drawings actually installed in the field. There were rows where the pipes turned up so that you could tell that was where the walls were and that the pipes were for electrical outlets. There were also pipes in the middle of nowhere that must have been for floorboxes. I just thought this was the greatest thing. I was so proud, I made a print of one of my drawings and brought it home to put on the wall in my room. I actually took that plan with me to show my friends and relatives what I was doing. Oh, to be naive and energetic like that again.

Two days after I visited the field, a directive was sent to all the subcontractors on the Mt. Sinai project from the Diesel Construction Company's Vice President and General Superintendent, Arthur Nusbaum, which actually said that women were not to be allowed on the construction site. The letter said that their hairdos were not conducive to wearing hardhats and their foot wear was inappropriate and dangerous, as were their skirts and dresses. In 1971, women were not allowed to wear pants to most normal jobs. For that matter, women were not allowed to wear pants to certain restaurants. So it was a reasonable conclusion that a "woman" would be wearing a skirt and high heels and would have "done" hair. I was officially banned from the site. (August 1971)

Of course, this was pure unadulterated bullshit. My hair was long and flat, I didn't have a hairdo. My hardhat fitted on my head perfectly, and my shoes were more appropriate than the oxfords and loafers the big shots wore when they walked around in their fancy suits. I didn't wear a skirt and no woman in her right mind would wear a skirt if she was going to walk a construction site. This was just about keeping women off the site. It was really about two things. First, it was about keeping women in their place. Just like the rules requiring to wear skirts in the office kept women in their place. Second, it was the result of some genius (probably Nusbaum) getting the idea that women in the field might distract the men or make them feel self-conscious about pissing on columns. For whatever reason, the directive was crystal clear, no women in the field.

I would run into this prohibition twice again before I was set free to go out in the field and take my sexual harassment as I chose to in the late 70s.

I stayed at Zwicker for the rest of the summer and when I left they threw a big lunch for me. I loved that job. I loved Al Silverman because he was fair to me. After one of the pours, we learned that there were a lot of conduits missing the wall, (coming out of the slab in the wrong place) and it was a floor I drew up. This prick, one of the full time assistants, blamed me for it, insisting I be fired. (Of course, any error reflected on Al, too.) Al got to the bottom of the matter and found out there was a revision to the plan, made after I had done the slab drawing, and all my dimensions were correct – all of them. We would be paid in full for any changes that had to be made. Al thought I was cute but he was always like a big brother. Al was the salt of the earth. I loved the job, but I had to go back to school and finish my degree.

I made friends with a lot of people for different reasons. When you are young and cute, people will tend to like you if you are not obnoxious. I was friendly and I worked like a dog. What's not to like? Later, the same group would not be so gracious. Most of all, I got friendly with the engineer who pasted the vanity panel on my desk the first day. He was only a year and a half older than me and smoking hot, or so I thought. But we were just friends because I had a steady boyfriend, which is always good to say because it lets you get out of all sorts of situations, but if you end up cheating, hey, it's not like you're married or engaged or anything.

After I left, I missed Al so much. And of course, Pete, the young engineer, who I lusted over and the rest of the people at Zwicker, the boss's secretary and the receptionist and the other draftsmen. After about two weeks, I got a call from Al asking if I could work part time when I was not in class. This was like the answer to a prayer because I needed the money and also because I wanted to see Pete. So I went back to work two afternoons a week and Saturdays.

I had been seeing someone else for a long time, so, even though I had a crush on Pete, I never did anything with him except walk up to the pizza place on Friday and, of course, flirt like crazy. After I left Zwicker, I thought about him, but I never tried to call him. When I went back to Zwicker, my crush was still alive and grew with every day. Meanwhile, my boyfriend was off at law school and started to give me a hard time because his mother hated me and wanted us to break up. So I wasn't seeing him so much even though he lived a mile away from me.

One Friday, I was working late, and Pete always worked late, so we both left work at the same time and he invited me out for a drink. Or maybe I invited him. Same difference. The point is by the end of the night we were making out. He didn't want me going home alone on the subway so we took the train together to his home in the Bronx and I met his mom and sister and nieces. Then he got his car and drove me home. We got home at around 2:00AM and, naturally, my father was awake. So my dad asked Pete to have coffee, which he did and started talking about being an electrical engineer and working for an electrician. My father always waited up for me. It didn't really bother me, but I felt sorry for him because sometimes I came in pretty late. Anyway, this night, in the middle of coffee, my father disappears. He comes back a few minutes later with a blender and asks Pete if he could fix it. Pete said, "Sure." And took the blender. I was pretty certain that Pete would stand on his head and do anything he could in the world, including bringing it to a repair place, but he was going to fix that blender. Pete was incredibly stuck on me. That night was a life change for the three of us. The next day I drove up to Pete's house in the Bronx and hung out with his sister and nieces while he did chores, including fixing the blender. Then, in the early evening, Pete came to my house with the fixed blender. Me, my dad, and Pete were forevermore sold on each other.

    This was, to my recollection, the best time of my life, (tied with my trip to Europe in 1969). I can hear a song that was popular at the time, like Ron Stewart's "Maggie May" and be transported right back there. I was never so alive. I thought the world was just a fabulous place. I was so incredibly happy.

On the other hand, I was barely scraping by at school. For the very first time in my life, I started skipping classes. And I had a problem at home. During the summer, my brother moved back home with his wife and her boy and was staying at my mother's house. At first I was very happy about this but after a while, it became hard to handle. I had set up my room really nice, with my slab drawing on the wall, but I also had a bookcase and a color TV that I bought with Macy money. At the time, my parents only had a black and white TV. I let my brother use my room. One night he spilled beer all over my bookcase and soaked some of my engineering books. That was the last straw. I decided to move out.

I found an apartment with my two friends. We had three bedrooms in a two-family on Liberty Avenue under the elevated train. I didn't even have a bed, I had a folding cot. A real bed was one of the first things I bought with my part-time Zwicker money. I was working a lot, including Saturdays. I was spending all my free time with Pete. Besides a bed, we didn't have a lot of things. For instance, there was no refrigerator in the apartment. Pete was always bringing me things like a coffee pot or flowers. One day he brought me an old refrigerator that he had in his basement. It worked, and my roommates Jeanne and Margaret painted it brown to match the kitchen. Another time, he came in and announced that he had bought me a car. Al Silverman had a friend who helped me get cheap insurance and I had, courtesy of Pete's friend, a teacher at a vocational technical high school where the kids fixed up old cars and sold them, a 1960 Ford Fairlane. The best thing about that car was it had a column shifter, which I learned in a minute because I knew how to drive a stick, and none of my friends could drive it. So while I drove them everywhere, I didn't have to lend the car out. I had been borrowing my father's car, which was my sister's car before she went to California, but this gave me another kind of freedom. It was great to have my own car.

      Right after I started seeing Pete, I broke up my relationship with the other man. He was being tormented by his mother and the rigors of law school. It was the right thing to do. It was very obvious that Pete and I were getting serious. We started talking about getting married. He was helping support his mother, and he had nothing, and I had nothing. I was still in school. But we got married. We borrowed $500 from Al Silverman to put up the deposit on an apartment and on December 30, 1971 we went to City Hall and tied the knot. We moved to Brooklyn.

Chapter 3 - The Real World

I continued to work at Zwicker for a while and then we decided I should just focus on finishing school. The atmosphere had changed precipitously because I had gotten married. First thing, the accountant made me change my name on the payroll. I did not want to do this, I wanted to keep my name. At first Pete went along with it, but as I pushed harder and harder, he started to feel bad. The accountant who insisted on making my checks out with the married name was asking Pete what was wrong with me, and why didn't he just insist I use his name? We were just kids, and we had a tremendous amount on our plate – my school, not having much money, just being married and getting used to it, having to help support his mother, who also was not crazy about me. I just capitulated and changed my name. That is how it happened.

People were treating me differently in other ways too. It was as if they did not like me as much. The project team moved out to the field in January and I went too as part of the team. The general contractor did not make a fuss about that because I was in a shanty on the ground floor, not walking the job. But it was very cold in the shanty, I had to do drafting with a coat and gloves on, and it was hard and not fun. Nothing seemed fun anymore, and certainly not work. Pete and I decided it would be best for me if I just concentrated on finishing school. Of course, the kids at school all treated me differently too, now that I was married.

This was probably my first experience with depression but I thought it was related to taking birth control pills. I ended up reverting to being a child. We spent every weekend at Pete's mom's house and she did our laundry and treated me like another daughter. I liked being there and I loved Pete's sister and nieces. But I was very blue. When I finished college, and I managed to get through just fine, I didn't go to graduation. When I think about this I still get very sad. I had sort of stopped caring. I didn't think I was special anymore.

After graduation I went back to Zwicker but they did not put me on the Mt. Sinai project. Instead they brought me into the office and assigned me to work for a man who was trying to come up with a way to computerize the business. The high point of my job was carrying his punch cards to a central office on 59th St so he could get a computer printout. There were very few large computers at the time, companies shared them. Today equipment with the capability of that computer, the IBM 360/70, could fit on a chip.

I stopped wearing skirts altogether. I had no reason, I guess I was more comfortable in slacks. I still cared about the way I looked, I wore makeup and everything, and then I didn't. At some point I stopped combing my hair. It was really very long and especially in the back, it was just like a hornet's nest. It's funny because when I finally got it cut, I remember the stylist yelled at the washer because she washed my hair without cutting it, so he had to try to work through the tangles before it could be cut properly.

It's hard to tell how I fell into this rut but I think it had something to do with my work situation. While I was still in school, I was kind of a "hot babe", even though I wore pants, I had a big chest and wore t-shirts and they were all enthralled by me because I was also a freak. A girl who was studying engineering. But when I graduated two things happened at the same time.

First, I got married. Worse yet, I married someone from work. So even though I was still cute, no one could think about me that way because I was Pete's wife. So I went from being the really hot girl who was going to engineering school, to the wife of someone everyone knew.

The second bad thing was my graduating was the end of the promise. There was no work for engineers that year, and the only choice I had was to keep the crappo job I had working with my husband on shit. Well, he worked on cool stuff, but I worked on shit. No more drafting or slab drawings. I was kept away from anything that related to the field at all. The great promise just blew up like a bubble. Now I was being asked to make copies. I was a girl sitting outside the door of the chief estimator's office and everyone that entered or left that office asked me to make copies.

I had kept that job right after Pete and I got married because we needed the money. I was still in school but had 2 days without classes. As a condition to getting married, I made my husband promise me that I would get to finish school. It was so important to me to finish. So I stayed in school for that last semester – and worked. My whole crew was sent off to the field office at Mt. Sinai Hospital. I was really good at what I had been doing so they were letting me do new stuff. I was learning and I felt good about it. But it was cold as a bitch in that shanty. And I had to do my drafting with gloves on. I only worked a few hours a week, but by the end of the first week, an order came down from the General Contractor forbidding subcontractors from having female employees on the site. Period. So I was sent back to the office. Where I would have nothing to do but grunt work.

I think this was the beginning of the spiral that ended with the uncombed hair. It was the beginning of a depression. I was nobody. I went from being on top of the world to being nobody. I was somebody's wife - that's all. I couldn't even keep my name. The pay clerk at the office insisted in making my checks out in my married name. There were no laws to protect me. Hell, there was no law that stopped them from throwing me off the job. Pete and I decided I should quit - at least until I finished school. And I did. But I was already lost. My friends at school treated me differently now that I was married, and my husband treated me really differently. He was all over me. I couldn't call any of my male friends or even talk about them. He wouldn't let me go to any parties, even though he was invited too. We were too young. He stopped me from wearing clothes that made me look sexy and I started to feel like nothing. I gained weight. We lived in a tiny apartment in Brooklyn that was always a mess and I spent most of my time at Pete's mom's house with his sister and my nieces who were close in age. I truly lost my sense of self. My best friend in the world, my sister, moved to California and I just lost my bearings. When graduation day finally came, I just stayed home. It really didn't matter anymore.

So that was the beginning. Then hearing about how a woman could never do this or do that, didn't help me. Feeling ugly and fat and ultimately like nothing.

I lost my way but not my fight. I kept the anger and even though it sounds trite, Ms. helped. The magazine and the appellation. I started using it right away. After working for over a year, my welcome at Zwicker had pretty much run out. My being there hurt both myself and my husband's career. People didn't like me for what I was. Pete would have gone farther, if he had a normal wife. I asked for a raise once, and the boss told me he would give my raise to my husband. I am not making this up. I had no one to complain to, no one to talk do. The bastard of a slave driver didn't pay Pete very well either. He sent Pete to work in Philadelphia and we didn't see each other all week long.

One day, I decided I would get a credit card. Not a chance. Not in my name. So I decided to borrow money. Back in those days it was called a personal loan. I tried to borrow $500. I was turned down flat. Reason - married woman.

That was the reason. Not lack of income - I was a graduate engineer and I made more money than your average clerk or salesman. No, I was actually told that I could easily become pregnant and that would be the end of my income. I was a bad risk. This was routine then. A woman's income did not count in a mortgage application. A married woman of childbearing age was nothing.

New York was progressive and there were laws on the books. I knew it but didn't know where to begin. Somehow I found the Human Rights Commission. They took up my cause. The bank said they would give me the loan if my husband co-signed. We are still talking about $500 here. I thought I should just do it to build up my credit and then I said goddammit, no. A man with a degree and a year and a half of work experience and a passbook savings account (which of course I closed when I got married) would get a lousy stinking $500 loan! I held my ground and got the loan. Then I got a credit card with a $500 limit which grew steadily. I fought for everything in my life and I fought for that stupid loan (with the HRC's help.)

At Zwicker, I had some friends and some people who actually respected me. All the men were male chauvinists because all the men in the world were male chauvinists at that time, but a few of them were sexist bastards who either really believed women were inferior or just hated women, and they came down on me picking at me for every possible thing. Al Silverman had died of a heart attack and Pete was away in Philly. It came to a point where I was chastised so badly that I just wanted to quit. Pete supported me in this and it gave me great pleasure to quit the day before the company Christmas Party. I remember that night the band played a cover of "I am Woman", the Helen Reddy anthem to the young feminist movement, and I jumped and screamed and sang out with the wives of the bastards who were holding me back. That was the turn of 1973 and the beginning of a very tough two years.

One of my heroes, our general superintendent, who loved me from the time I was the hot girl through the days I was just Pete's wife, the graduate engineer who made copies for vendors visiting the chief estimator. He helped me find a job with a top contractor, Fischbach and Moore, Inc.

They hired me as an estimator. I was the only engineer in the department and one of three engineers in the entire company.

The big difference between Fischbach and Zwicker was that Pete didn't work there. So people could say anything they wanted to me or about me without breaking any code among men.

This is where it really took off - in the estimating department at Fischbach. There were these two men. The chief estimator was an overblown wanna-be engineer who never got past freshman year but was a smart and hardworking thirty something guy who had the hots for me no matter how I deteriorated. The other guy was an old fuck. A skinny wiry sleazy so called expert estimator - he was an old Navy guy - maybe Seabees, and he worked electrical forever, and knew everything. When the boss wasn't around and we weren't busy this guy, Hertenstein, would hold court and all the guys in the department would gather around to listen to all his war stories, not about real war, just war stories about the business. And we would be sitting there and out of nowhere, he would just attack me. I know, it sounds ridiculous, even preposterous that this could happen even once, but it happened so many times. He would start out with something like "why did you study engineering?", and then "why are you working in contracting which is man's work?", and then finally, why do you want to be a man? "What is wrong with you? You are a freak." And no one would defend me and I couldn't get away, until he just stopped. And I went home and cried and felt like shit and started hating myself. And I stopped combing my hair again. See Paul, the chief estimator, would not let this happen in front of him. But I never went to him, just like it took me months to tell my mother that Mary Ellen and Billy were punching me in the stomach every day, or to tell the nuns that the boys were making a spectacle of my boobs in the eighth grade. And while telling was all it took to end my other travails, I didn't tell anyone about Hertenstein. I just got past him. He became irrelevant. He was a wizened bitter and wicked old man who couldn't abide with a woman surpassing him. He was the assistant chief estimator and he could trick himself into believing that he was something important until a 23 year old girl entered his life, who was a real engineer.

(This kind of emotional torture was heaped upon me again, and although I was wiser, it still got to me. I was called a dyke a lot, even though I was married. I always hated that word because it is misogynistic. Guys think all strong women are gay and guys hate gay women because they don't need men. Guys would say my husband was not a real man, that he was pussywhipped, and that he couldn't even control a woman. I didn't go back to Pete with this because I didn't know what he would do. I didn't want to give up my job or my marriage.)

I languished in estimating at Fischbach for the time I was there, but every now and then I got a shot at the big time. I did most of the estimating work on a job at Irving Trust Bank, now long gone, and we got the job. So they let me be the project manager. It was a renovation job. I got to work with a foreman named Kingman, who liked me. Maybe because I was honest. This guy was a forerunner tea party type, although he was not an asshole. But he wore a coat made from a deer he killed himself and drove an American which is the brand of the car. He was a good foreman, smart. Here is a great side story. We were working in the ceiling and there was very little space between the framing and the ductwork. We needed to get someone between and there was this tiny Puerto Rican kid who fit the bill. He was a real hero to us, but it never occurred to these guys that an ordinary sized woman could have accomplished the same herculean feat.

Anyway, Irving Trust was big coup for me. The down side was that I had to entertain the Vice President. In 1974 that meant one thing — no, not that! The three martini lunch, and this guy was a fish. All I remember was being horrifically bored, but he signed the extras.

I was such a gonif when it came to extras. I used to say that subcontractors were like the gypsies who stole the nails from Christ's corpse. We got a pass from the almighty for the sin of stealing. I guess the logic was that the general contractors and owners were like the Romans. Anyway, I made a lot of money for Fischbach on change orders.

Still I was back in the estimating department for the majority of the time. We got a shot at an enormous project - the Moscow World Trade Center. We did a joint venture bid with F&M Systems which was a sister company that did complex electronic system installations that a five year old would laugh at now. We bid systems and electric work. One of the things we needed to do was entertain the Russians, who were like kids in a candy store, and bulls in a china shop all at the same time. There was this one guy. My boss called him Cochise because he had a Mohawk haircut. (Not popular at the time). His name was Yuri. He was a dog. Really. He loved me. He loved all the American women and he loved his vodka. The Russians lived in this mansion in the Bronx, which the government rented out for all of their envoys. This was during the height of the KGB era. These guys literally could not talk. Half of them were spies. You didn't know which was which, but the spies were spying on the spies.

We would have these marathon meetings going from 8:00 in the morning to 10:00 at night and then they would want to be entertained. My people really gave me a lot of crap about this Yuri. It was a big joke, that I should take one for the team. Obviously, I didn't want any part of him. The hysterical thing is that the Russians went out one night and he actually got in trouble. He got a little too friendly with a bar waitress and there was a scene in this club, cops, etc. He actually got sent back home and the story made the tabloids. For all I know they sent him to Siberia. What a creep. The job was bid on a unit price basis with probably a thousand unit price items. We had to put an add and a delete number in for each task. The way that works is the base job has a finite number of say duplex outlets. So we get paid our unit price for that number and the total contract amount was based on the quantities of every different element times the unit price for it. Then, if there was a change to the plans later on, we would either have to add or delete the amount of items being changed multiplied by the agreed upon unit price. So the trick was to scour the documents and figure out what there was not enough of and what there was too much of and adjust the unit prices up and down so that at the end we would get the greatest amount of money. Simple concept - where we determined there would be deductions the price would be unusually low, and where we decided there was not enough of something on the plans, they would pay a much higher price. I was good at this kind of forensic work.

My big perk was a trip to Texas. Dallas. That is where the headquarters of F&M Systems was. I was supposed to meet with my counterparts there and go over the prices for all of the systems items. I was accompanied by (in that I met up with) the engineer for the project. I was there for two days. I got to fly first class for the very first time in my life. It's funny, but all of the people in the office were excited about this. Back then, many people had never flown, not to mention first class. They told me to look out for Dallas Cowboys, as if I would know one if I fell over him. This was the first one of a lifetime of business trips for me.

The people in Dallas really got a kick out of me. A girl engineer. Plus my New York accent! We worked long and hard and then went out, Omigod, I wanted to go to sleep. They called themselves Dallasites. I asked them if that was like parasites - they thought I was hysterical. Crazy, Dallasites! They all wanted to go out and have a good time with the girl engineer. I don't remember too much about that trip, although I learned a lot of stuff about electronics that which had me totally dazzled. Meanwhile, at best, it was the functional equivalent to an abacus compared to today's computers, but it was cutting edge and interesting. What I do remember is there was another trip.

As a result of the work we did in NY and Dallas, Fischbach made the short list. We were called to Moscow. Except, I, personally, didn't make the final cut. It's kind of like the reverse of that song Dance 10 Looks 3 in A Chorus Line when the girl doesn't get the job because she is not good looking. I didn't get to go to Russia because I was a girl and my looks were good enough for my boss to be all over me. They didn't think it was worth the risk, sending a married girl away with a letch. This trip was something I earned. I deserved to go, and I was denied it, and for one reason only. I should have seen the writing on the wall, right then and there with this company, because this pattern would ultimately repeat itself and lead to my quitting. But more on that later. The upshot of the Russia trip was we got the job. How I found out of this was I was in the coffee room at Fischbach and the letch came flying in and grabbed me and kissed me on the lips to convey the good news – yuck. It was some time before I learned that the letch, that is the chief estimator, had long before put out the word that he had been sleeping with me.

Fischbach was one of the major contractors in the country. It turned out though that it was not exactly clean. Along with a few other big name electricians it conspired to fix prices. Of course everyone thinks that contractors are all crooks, but I never thought that. People all think that contractors are all Italians. But these guys were

Jewish, as were the owners of Zwicker. But hell, people think all engineers are guys, right. So, at a time my former boss, not the letch but his boss, more of a lush than a letch, ended up taking the fall and went to jail. For now, I was still in the estimating department. And while I was there, Fischbach ruled and we got some very high profile work.

We got a humongous job – the Citicorp Center, the one on 53rd and Park. Half the office was assigned to it. I had worked in estimating with Leigh Scotti, who was given the job as Project Manager. He was probably the best PM Fischbach ever had, although not an engineer. For that matter, there were only two actual engineers at our shop and I was one of them. The assistant chief Estimator was not an engineer, and I didn't realize until long after that time, that the reason he hated me so much was partly because I was one. This is the guy who tortured me, the little sailor, Hertenstein.

Scotti wanted me on the job in the field. I was doing estimates for change orders for him. The change orders on Citicorp were legion, as I would later learn. Mountains of requests sat in piles at the general contractor's office. But we were told to proceed with the work and the change orders kept being processed, by me. Scotti made his move. First he consulted with his foreman, who liked me despite of being female, and got his permission. Then he consulted my boss who discussed the subject with his boss (the future felon) and maybe even the big boss (the guy the felon took the fall for) and it all was set. I was moving to the field. Does this sound familiar? Out of nowhere comes the Fucking Union in the body of John O'Malley, the General Superintendent, who said, "NO WOMEN IN THE FIELD." This time it was because it would make the men uncomfortable. And that was it.

Lots of people were pissed off about this, not just me, because I would have done a great job in the field. Continuing my habit of not sticking around where I was not appreciated, I quit this job. I tried to collect unemployment and the company denied me. Nowadays, I would have a great lawsuit. Back then leaving a job because you were discriminated against was not a good enough reason for the unemployment office.

So I had no job and no income.

Chapter 4 - The Field

My friend Artie Nusbaum came to the rescue. He was the Project Manager on Citicorp Center. This is the same Artie that got me kicked off the Mt. Sinai project, my sister's friend.

Artie said that extra work orders and requests were building up on the Citicorp project and he needed someone who could check them for accuracy and then process them for payment. Since I was an electrical estimator he thought I could take care of the Fischbach change orders and he also thought he could show me how to check the other trades. I was somewhat familiar with architectural drawings and needed a job badly but I was worried about the ethics of reviewing Fischbach's extras since I had inside knowledge of their estimating procedures. Then I said to myself, what are you nuts? They fucked you over, all you are going to do is make sure they aren't stealing.

So in one of the many ironies of my life, I ended up working in the field at Citicorp Center and no one cared. Except for that sonofabitch Irishman who should burn in hell.

What is fascinating is how Fischbach took my working for HRH. They were thrilled. Yes, it was likely that I was going to call them on overestimates, and overbilling, but they also knew that I was a hard worker and once someone actually went over their change orders and approved them, there was a chance they would get paid. Some of this stuff had been sitting around for over two years and was growing into the millions. Within weeks of my starting my review, checks began rolling out.

My job was to check several things. First the work had to be extra and not part of the contract. Then it had to be measured in terms of quantity, which meant comparing one set of plans to another. On Citicorp the plans were past revision number 20. That means 20 different plans had been issued for each floor, therefore virtually every trade had change order requests for each of these plans. In all, we probably had a few thousand plans. Each time a plan was changed, almost every system was affected. For instance if a wall was moved, the electric was moved and lighting and perhaps doors, maybe HVAC if there was a vent in that wall. If the wall was already up when it was relocated then there was the cost of taking down the old wall and reinstalling the new one. Lots of times I didn't know whether the work had been done before the change and had to ferret that information out by talking to the people supervising the work in the field. If the work wasn't done, and the change was minor, there would be no cost. On the other hand, if something had to be removed and reinstalled, it could be expensive. This was very complex business.

Once I had the electrical nearly caught up, Artie put me to the other trades. Some of this was fairly easy, but most of it was a new world for me. I had to learn plumbing, hvac, and sprinkler. But guess what? These subcontractors were suffering like Fischbach had been with years of backlog in change orders and they were desperate to have them looked at. It was in their interest to work with me and they did. They taught me their trades! I learned how to read plumbing drawing from plumbers, I learned HVAC from tinknockers and pipefitters and I learned the sprinkler trade from the sprinkler fitters. Artie and the assistant project managers helped me out too. I was so willing to learn, and there was mountains of work for me to do, so it was really a lot of fun and rewarding. Plus all of a sudden I had a lot of power.

Even though I did not know the other trades, I could figure out how to labor the work. One of the things I did was watch the work being done. And I had access to estimating manuals and also the mechanical and general supers who spent the day in the field observing work. Plus everyone was willing to help me and I wanted to learn.

I covered everything. The only thing I really struggled with was structural steel although I was able to check the plan revisions on that as well.

There was one caveat to all this, and that was, Artie said it was only going to be a temporary position, just until the change orders were reviewed. I had been looking for work and one of the jobs I applied for was at Con Edison, our local utility. I got a call from them and went for an interview. I got the job. So after working about 3 months at Citicorp, and having the time of my life, it was time to go back to work and take a real job, because I could not rely on HRH.

I went to Con Ed. I was sent to work in the estimating department. My first assignment was to work on developing labor units for transmission line work. I can hardly remember anything about Con Ed. The pay was good, better than Fischbach and HRH. But I really didn't know what they wanted me to do and felt lost. I would sit in the library and look at books about transmission lines. There were four or five others in the department and most of them seemed lost too. The difference was it didn't seem to bother them, and it was making me crazy. Each day was like a hundred hours long. I had just come from the Wild West where everything was go go go and now it was slow slow slow. Con Ed was all about manana. About a week after I started, I was sent to Indian Point, the nuclear power plant in upstate New York, to qualify for a clearance. To this day, I can't imagine why I needed this clearance. All the management people got cleared for high level access. But at least it was one day break from the boredom of working there in the office. I requisitioned a car, one of those blue compacts you see around with Con Ed written in white. I drove up to Indian Point and took a class in radiation safety, stuff like that. Afterwards, I took a test, passed and was given a really high level clearance to come into and move around the plant freely.

Back in the library, I languished. I was constantly talking to my HRH friends on the phone, and Artie said I could come back any time, but he was only promising I would have a few months' work. I finally couldn't take it anymore. I was dreaming about Citicorp. I hated Con Ed. I finally quit. No one could believe that I had actually quit my job. (In fact, this was the 3rd job I quit in my young life.) It had only been 5 weeks. Within days, everyone on the floor knew about me and I became a bit of a legend at Con Ed because it seems everyone hated it, but I was the only they ever saw with the guts to just walk out.

Everyone was thrilled to see me back at Citicorp. The subs were cheering. I went back to my former task of change orders which continued to grow by leaps and bounds. When the numbers were so high, the officials at Citibank started asking questions and I was given the opportunity to defend my work to the bosses. In retrospect, I was really the only one who knew anything about what I was doing, and I had it really under control. Besides being tough on Fischbach, I kicked everyone else's asses too. When I was finished with a $40,000.00 change order, it was more like $20,000.00, but you could bet that every foot of wire, or gallon of paint, or pound of tin was right on the money. So when I got to appear before the Sr. VP of Citibank, I was well armed and confident.

This was the beginning of an ethic I developed which got me into trouble down the line, but I never wavered on. I would not cheat a subcontractor. Once we agreed on an amount there were no more haircuts. I beat the hell out of an extra and there was only one shot. Otherwise, why would the other side ever be willing to negotiate? I remember what I said when Bob Dexter, the Vice President, told me that he did not like what he was seeing. I told him "I have a responsibility to my subs". This came out of nowhere, but I believed it. And it worked. He never questioned me again. It helped that Artie secretly told him that I killed the subs and no one could ever do better, but I never thought I bested anyone, only that we reached a fair and honest solution.

After the building was pretty much completed, we moved in to offices on one of the floors and it was really nice there. Of course, I still loved what I was doing. I was focusing a lot of time on the Building Management System now. The BMS is a master control system that monitors and controls virtually everything mechanical on the job. If you had a mechanical valve open, the BMS would know it and if that was opened for a reason, the BMS would respond. For Example a low flow alarm would tell a pump to put more water into a tank. It was complex but relatively easy to follow. Each floor had a panel and each panel, hundreds of connections. My job was to observe the progress in the field. I did a lot of talking with electricians which drove that Irishman Superintendent nuts, and he was constantly complaining about me, but that did not phase Artie, because he knew I was doing my job. Fischbach was billing for the installation, and I was making sure it got done.

One of the interesting things about Citicorp is it has a massive block of concrete on the top of the building that moves in reaction to wind forces but it is controlled electronically as part of the BMS. This was called the tuned mass damper. Its purpose was to compensate for swaying which happens at the top of all tall buildings. It also saved the company millions in structural costs.

The steel design for structural integrity itself, was not related to the TMD, the building had to stand on its own. The TMD only reacted to the swaying. At a point in time, it was learned that the engineer had used the wrong calculations when the building was designed and it was at risk structurally if there was a hundred year storm. This is a building department and best practices criteria. The new information showed that the building could potentially collapse.

Apparently the joints were originally to be welded, that it was changed to bolts. It is the bolting that was not sufficient as designed to absorb potential wind loading. What transpired is an incredible story about an engineer with real integrity and a group of people working together to solve a problem. My part was just as an observer. Certain of the steel columns required repair. HRH had to tear finished offices apart and weld H shaped pieces of steel on certain of the joints in the steel members. All the work was done at night. We were under pressure to avoid the hurricane season. Amazingly, it got done. Meanwhile, the damper is still in place doing its job to compensate for the swaying. Eventually, I got to check and negotiate all of the change orders for putting the walls and finishes back together.

Chapter 5 - The Hyatt - Be Careful What You Wish For

A lot of the Citicorp crew was sent over to work on the renovation of the old Commodore Hotel on 42nd Street and I went along. I was now called an assistant project manager, and it was a permanent position. The top floor of the empty hotel had offices in it and the project staff occupied them. The owner of the project was a joint venture between Hyatt Hotels and Donald Trump. This hotel was supposed to be called the Hyatt Regency, but because there was a Regency Hotel in NY on 61st Street, they changed the name to the Grand Hyatt and it would be the first of several of the Hyatt Grand brand.

Nusbaum was now the head of field operations for HRH, and he became my mentor. The hotel was a mess, literally. There were vagrants living in the boiler room which was off the lobby of Grand Central Station and could be broken into and it was incredibly warm so it was a big draw for these homeless souls. Partly as a result, the room was crawling with lice, and we had a hard time getting the union workers to do anything in there. This was just one of the many problems. We had rats as big as cats living in the hotel basements. We brought in cats and the rats killed them. We also had holdouts from the Single Room Occupancy days which Trump's people had to dispatch along with some tenants and a handful of hookers, who eventually returned to service the construction workers.

This was Donald's first job and he was very hands on. His intention was to salvage everything that could be saved, which turned out to be a really bad decision because we spent so much money going around things, and fixing things, that a complete gut would have been cheaper and faster. This kind of error gets made because you have the deadly combination of an aggressive and powerful person in charge, who is also inexperienced. The architects were afraid to challenge him, and the GC just went along figuring they would get paid for all the changes. But everyone including HRH underestimated this project.

Although I worked for Artie, there was a Project Manager that I reported to, Ed Sullivan, and there were other officers at HRH who were also my bosses and the President of the company, Irving Fisher. The first time I met Irv, he was at the job. He handed me a copy of the contract and said, "read this and learn it. I want you to make sure that every thing that gets done on this job that is not in this contract is recorded and paid for. These people will kill you. Keep records of everything." Wow. What an introduction. It was obvious right then and there that Fisher knew that this job was going to cost a hell of a lot more than the $37 million guaranteed price and we were going to have to fight tooth and nail for every cent. We expected litigation from the get go.

As it turned out there were too many changes to keep track of. You would have to stop the job cold, do a new design and bid it out all over. Instead, the construction contract was revised to a construction management contract or a cost plus. The subcontracts would be on a fixed price but HRH would be paid a fee plus its cost for general labor and general conditions. This change dramatically improved relations with Donald, although it did not keep him from getting in the way, and making decisions that would cost the project money. When completed, The Grand Hyatt cost more than twice the original budget, but Hyatt and Donald made a fortune and everyone was happy.

The original hotel was very old. It had been one of the most luxurious in the city, but had long fallen into disrepair as had the general East 42nd Street area. The Commodore was more like a flop house on top of Grand Central Station which itself had fallen on hard times and was in serious disrepair.

The entire exterior of the building had to be redone. Donald chose to update it with a glass curtain wall. The guest rooms were too small for a modern hotel. We had to tear down walls and combine three rooms to make two, so the rooms would be marketable. We ended up mostly gutting the public spaces, but we saved a lot of pipes and we saved all the steel structure, although much of it had to be repaired.

The first thing HRH did was identify what was to be saved and what was to be removed by spray painting a red mark on it if it was going, a green mark if it was staying, a yellow mark if it was going later and a blue mark if it belonged to

ConRail, which was the owner of Grand Central. I arrived at the job site just as demolition was underway.

My office was the Hotel's old money counting room. It was tiny and it was tucked into a corner of the structure and there was a concrete shelf behind the desk. The door was steel and the walls were all concrete. It was like Fort Knox.

One of my first jobs was to do the requisition. Every month each subcontractor would submit an invoice for the work it had completed. Although the work end date was the last day of the month, we needed to get the papers in about 10 days before that so they could be reviewed and negotiated. At first, I just got the finally agreed payments, later I did the negotiations.

Before the project started, each contractor would submit a schedule of values. That was a breakdown of all the different elements of the project and how much each was worth. This schedule would be reviewed and approved by the general contractor and often changed. As the Assistant PM on the Hyatt, I made some after the fact changes. On my later projects, I negotiated these trade payment breakdowns for the owner, directly. The schedule of values is the first real dance that the Owner or GC does with the subs. The subs try to put higher values on work that will be done earlier in the project so they can "get ahead" of the project, meaning that they will be paid more than they spent. It is called front loading. This could make the difference between making or losing money on a job for a contractor. Margins are so tight on competitively bid projects that a few late payments can put a job in the red. So when you review a schedule of values, you should do it with a light hand, not with the intention of having subs finance the project, which some owners do, but I never did, and Trump never did, when I was in charge.

Every month the contractor sends in a bill with a percentage amount written next to the finally agreed schedule of values. This is the second dance, and here it is appropriate to be a bit sterner. Billing for work that is not done yet is the same thing as front loading and it is easy to get away with because there are so many values and so many alternatives. Work items are broken down by floor, and sometimes separated out for labor and material. When done properly, reviewing a requisition is very time consuming and difficult, and the subs rely on not being checked so thoroughly.

After the requisition is verified, and negotiated if necessary, the sub puts the final figures on the requisition and it is put into the master req that the general contractor makes. I put the requisition together for the Hyatt in the beginning. Eventually, we had a full time accountant who did this work, but for the time being, I would literally hole myself up in that vault of a room for two days and do the Construction Manager's Req. I liked doing this and it was important.

Other times, I did assistant project manager stuff. I checked estimates and change orders which I was now very experienced at, having done Citicorp Center. I also went over the plans when they came in to look at the changes to see how they would affect the work in progress. There were two other assistant PMs on the job and a superintendent and some assistant supers. As the job grew so did the staff.

By the time most of the demolition was done, we started getting shop drawings in and they needed to be coordinated. Depending the level of intricacy and detail, job coordination may need to be done more than once. Basically what coordination means is the act of making sure everything fits. When the architect and engineers first layout the job, they are supposed to coordinate everything. When the subs and GC make suggestions, coordination must be considered again during the bidding phase. Finally when the subs are ready to do the work they make shop drawings. Some trades can install their work from the architecturals, such as walls, painters, flooring. Other trades need to make their own drawings, using the contract plans as a guide only. On a very complicated project like the Hyatt, mechanical subcontractors always make full or partial shop drawings. Again, the engineers are supposed to check the shop drawings and so is the architect, but, except in cases of extreme conflicts which can be easily identified, plans are approved for final coordination in the field, and this is done directly by the subs under the supervision of the general contractor, with help from the consultants if needed.

Coordination had begun to an extent, meaning that the tinknocker (ductwork sub) had already begun fabricating ductwork and installing it, technically without permission. No meetings had been held yet but one was scheduled. We had a mechanical superintendent on the job. He was a mechanical engineer who had been with HRH for a very long time and they parked him at the Hyatt. One look would tell you he was not up to the job of coordinating this project. To coordinate this very complex project one had not only to understand the work of all the trades, but, more importantly you had to be able to sniff out bullshit and keep control over it. But the hardest part of coordination was making people make changes at their own cost. The basic understanding is that people would move to accommodate each other without causing a change to the structure or the architectural elements. It meant relocating pipes, flattening ducts, combining runs, uncombining runs, and in some cases abandoning work that was done prior to coordination. On a normal project this is difficult work, on a project like the Hyatt, it was a nightmare. Remember, per Donald, we had kept a lot of existing pipe, and all of the structure. Also we had the Conrail lines which were sacrosanct and could not be touched. Coordinating this project took someone with nerves of steel and a mouth that could resonate above all others. Artie took me aside and told me he was making me the mechanical superintendent. Of course, I still had to do the requisition.

The crew that did the coordination consisted of the toughest and biggest draftsmen the trades had. The tinknocker was a guy named Walash who was easily 6'3". The electrician was about 6' and he weighed a good 250 pounds. His name was Rocco. These were the two toughest guys and they had the biggest work and the most "hits". A hit occurs when two items occupy the same location. Every draftsman was also a journeyman too, that is an experienced mechanic, except for the Plumber who was a company executive. So I had a tinknocker, an electrician, two pipe fitters (hvac and sprinkler) and a big shot plumber, who was also a big guy, who made sexual innuendos about everything. Actually, the plumber was the only one who ever said anything to me off color and the other guys thought he was a jerk. Coordination was about the business only. If, at first, the coordinators had reservations about me, I soon won them over. We were dealing with time and money and there nothing to be gained by alienating me. I had the power.

The way it works is the largest trade puts his work on a reproducible drawing called a mylar. This is always the duct work. Then the next guy comes along and lays out his work, followed in turn by the others. Each uses a different color, brown, red, blue green and orange. Every time one crosses the other, at the same elevation, it is circled and called a hit. If a pipe or duct crosses a light fixture in the ceiling or hits a piece of existing steel that is also a hit.

Once the plan has been passed around to all the trades, there is a meeting to resolve the hits. Some hits are easy to fix. For example, pipes can be moved laterally fairly easily. However, when a ten inch line hits a steel beam, you usually can't work around it and have to bring in the structural engineer. Sometimes, you can cut the steel, if you are, for instance, right in the center of the web. Other times, it is a very big production involving reinforcing plates and welding and lots of money. My job was to avoid spending money and changing the architecture. For instance, you can always drop a ceiling. But that changes the aesthetics. Same thing with relocating a light. If the light is supposed to be in the center, you can move it to the side but it will look wrong. In a closet that might be OK. In a hallway it's a no-no. Sometimes you can substitute a light with a shallower box but most of the time, you either have to flatten the duct or relocate the pipe.

The beauty part of this was that I could learn as I went along because while one trade would say "There's nothing I can do," the other draftsmen would clue me into solutions. For instance, say a duct is running down a hall and there is a recessed light smack in the middle. The duct man says even if I hug the wall, I will still hit that light, it has to move. But another guy yells out make a pair of pants, and I say "pair of pants", like I know what the hell that is. A pair of pants means simply splitting the duct to go around an object. I learned so much and these guys were all experts, so it was a crash course in advanced construction.

My career was set in place when I was doing coordination. We had a terrible situation with the black iron duct on the first floor that exhausted the air of the restaurant's kitchens. It took up the entire ceiling space and nothing else could go in there. Normally, the solution would have been to reconfigure the duct and that was what I told the tinknocker to do. This man stood up and stared me down. Then he started cursing at me. At the same time, and the electrician who had to locate a big pull box in the same space was screaming at the tin man. It turned out this duct I wanted to reconfigure had already been fabricated. I famously told the tinknocker, "then throw the fucking thing out, and do it again the right way." This kind of thing happened a lot but this incident was the worst. Black iron duct is really really expensive. The guy told me "to go fuck yourself."

I didn't go to the PM with this, or the Superintendent. I went directly to Artie Nusbaum, the big boss. But I was too late. He had already gotten the call from General Sheet Metal. The owner of the company had told Artie I was incompetent and he had to remove me and threatened to go over Artie's head, if I wasn't taken off the coordination. From Artie's perspective, no one could have complimented me better. I stood up to this giant and did the right thing for the project. Artie told the tinknocker to throw out the duct. Now I don't know if some deal wasn't made to pay for some of the duct, because, as it turned out, the Superintendent had told General to go ahead without coordination and fabricate the duct, but that did not matter. For me, I was on the map now with a great future ahead of me. I was not to be screwed with.

The Hyatt jobsite was papered with disgusting nudie pictures all over the place. It was the very essence of a hostile environment. Initially there were three women on the site, myself, our job secretary who was a woman in her 50's who had been around and gave as good as she got, and a kid, around 20, who was secretary for the demolition guys. Her name was Anne. Everyone liked Anne. Anne tried to fight back in her own way. She bought a Playgirl calendar that had pictures of nude men and hung it over her desk. But that only invited more harassment because the guys would tease her about it. "Hey, you like that, you should see mine." It was probably the worst thing to do under the circumstances.

It was known on the job that I had a position with authority but that didn't stop the harassment. Men were constantly saying disgusting things to me and I tried to ignore it. But this one guy, a plumbing subforeman was way way way out of line. He was asking me out and hounding me, talking about my body and humiliating me in front of the other men. For the first time in my life, I reported something. I went to my boss, the Project Manager, Ed Sullivan, who was an Irish catholic. He recoiled at what I told him. He went to the plumber foreman and confronted him. The foreman blew it off. Sullivan took matter above the foreman to the Plumbing boss. I am sure my superintendent, Ronnie, was not supporting me at all. I wanted the guy removed from the job and initially Sullivan told me that would happen. The matter went higher than Sullivan though and the big bosses all decided this sub foreman was too important to the project to remove, and so he would stay but he had to apologize. The bastard never apologized to me but he left me alone after that. I learned from this incident, that even though I was more important to the project than some plumbing sub foreman, I had to pick my spots. And I didn't do any more complaining, although I endured a lot of shit.

Peeing on the columns was a thing guys like to do and they liked it better when I was around. I just ignored it. Any reaction at all on my part would have provoked more harassment. I did my best to pretend that I didn't see it. A lot of times I wanted to cry. But I didn't. Not on the job. Never. I felt lonely though, especially after the plumber incident. Even women who worked in the trades, had the union's grudging support. I was alone. I remember writing to Ms. Magazine and never hearing back. Ms. was a godsend to me but there was never a word in Ms. about female engineers, much less construction supervisors or workers. It was just not a fight Ms. wanted to pick. At the end of the day, wherever I was, for a long, long time, I was just me.

George Carlin, the late comedian, is famous for his seven dirty words sketch where he talks about words the FCC would not allow you to say on the air. I have my own seven dirty words list. Bitch, ballbuster, slut, whore, man-hater, dyke and cunt. Most of the time I was called one of these, it was preceded by the word fucking. This was both in front of my face and behind my back.

A good place to torment me was on the elevators. In the morning, and most of the day for that matter, the elevators were packed. One day I got on the elevator and my friend was there and he asked me where I had been, he hadn't seen me. I said I got in late this morning. He said "you got laid this morning." You would think he was Bob Hope from the laughter. "No, I got to work late." "No you said it, you got laid. I wish I got laid in the morning." And this was my friend.

Basically, the men on the job knew you could say whatever you wanted to me if the bosses weren't around and the prior experience told them that even if I report, it they will get away with it. It was still open season on me.

There were four types of men on the job – scary, creepy, banal and OK. Scary guys were the ones who threatened me, or were openly lascivious. Creepy guys were the leerers, and the ones who made gestures at me. Banal guys never bothered me, even if they gave me the eye, they were mostly harmless, except in a crowd. And there were the good guys who valued me and understood what was happening. One Project

Manager, Harold Jupiter was a guy like this. I don't even know what he was doing in construction, he seemed above it. He had a wife who was a professional and I think that had an influence on him. Or maybe it is the other way around, he was the type of man who would marry a woman who was, in all ways, his equal. Then there was my best friend on the job, Alex Crowder, who was a clean thinker, I don't think he ever considered a person's race or sex or religion as a factor in anything. And we carried on and said all sorts of things to each other without creating a shadow of a hard feeling, while getting a lot of laughs. See sexual harassment is nuanced, and that's part of the reason it's so hard to understand. Regardless of the situation, what I said, or what happened, Alex or Harold would never harass me.

Artie, who I idolized, harassed me all the time. One of his favorite things was to tell me I could not pee on a column. My retort was that I could pee on a beam. First I ignored him, then I would say so what, and the more used to it I became, the more I was willing to take him on. "You don't have the equipment," he said. This was penis talk, through and through. He knew I didn't like this. In ways, I was like the girl with the calendar. What was I supposed to do? Call him out on it? He was my boss, and my champion. I tried to blunt it. It was a no-win situation. Mostly this happened when we were just one on one, and I think he got his jollies out of it. I also believe that in his mind, this was a real limitation. Regardless, he gave me the same opportunities he would give a man. But, partly, the reason for this was I was smarter, harder working and more willing to make the work my life than most of the men he encountered. He would not have given the same opportunities to run of the mill women as he did to run of the mill men. Not by a long shot.

This is how it harassment works, it can be loud and ostentatious or it can be subtle and insidious. The big click heard around the world when Anita hill was harangued by the nasty Republican senators because she didn't just up and leave Clarence Thomas when he started bothering her, was the understanding of the nature of harassment and the need to endure it. The animals who tortured me (and that was *not* Artie) with "what kind of woman are you, do you want to be a man, do you have a dick," took the same approach as the senators. "If you don't like it why do you stay here?" "Go home and have a baby." "Women don't belong in construction." Verbally, or through my actions I said, "I want this job, and I will do what it takes." I shouldn't have had to stand for all the harassment, but now, at least, that has changed a lot. It would not have changed if I and a few others didn't bore through. My perseverance and my ambition are what got me to the heights I reached. But I guarantee there are diehards out there who still believe I was sleeping with the boss. They have to believe this because otherwise they would have to admit I was just better at my job than they were.

From the time I worked at Fischbach I had a bad back. The pains came and went but sometimes they were so bad that I couldn't stand straight. This usually happened when I got up from sitting for a long time. When we used to drive to work it would take me a few minutes to stand erect after getting out of our little Toyota. I would lean against the granite wall at Grand Central and just straighten out that way. Finally, it got so bad I had to have surgery.

I had a disc removed in January, 1979. I remember Artie coming to see me at the hospital with some other people from work. He told me I would never walk the scaffolds again. Truth was I hadn't walked the scaffold before either. The Hyatt was totally encapsulated with metal scaffolding and the exterior wall was installed off the scaffolds. I was hospitalized for 8 days and stayed home for another week. Two weeks after I had the surgery, I was back to work part time, that is, from 8:00AM to 2:00PM. Two weeks later I was full time. By then I had already been out on the scaffold with Artie.

Chapter 6 - A Position of Authority

Not long after my back surgery, I had the opportunity of a lifetime dropped in my lap. There was a guy, Howie, working for us as an assistant super. He was in charge of the 5th floor which housed the Ballroom, the Pre-function area and the catering and room service kitchen, which was enormous. The ballrooms could service up to 3000 people. It was one of the most important spaces in the building. The assistant super was recovering from a car accident and he walked with a limp. Artie thought he was good, but I didn't think he was any great shakes. He was always asking me to solve easy mechanical problems for me that he should have been able to handle himself.

Artie Nusbaum used to come to the job early in the morning once a week. He would walk the entire site with Sullivan and Ronnie, the Super, and, usually, Artie Miller, another VP from the company, would come along. If I was in the building, Artie would invite me along, so I made it my business to always be there. Walking a job with Artie was one of the greatest learning experiences you could have. Also I was able to run up my currency by being able to answer questions. Afterwards, we would have breakfast and I would tag along for that too. There were lots of assistants on the job, but I was the only one who would go to the trouble of being there for the walkthroughs although, I am not sure they would have been invited.

One day, Artie and Artie came to the job and Sullivan was there and we did the walkthrough. Then we went across the street for breakfast at Howard Johnson's. The Arties had a dilemma they had to share with Sullivan and resolve. Howie, the limp super, was getting a hard time from his lawyer for working and he had to quit. So now they needed to replace him, and they had to figure out how they could do this without slowing down the progress. Artie looked at me and said, "Can *you* do it?" Sullivan said nothing. I was totally shocked. I was never a super before, not even an apprentice, although I knew my way around the jobsite from checking requisitions and being the mechanical super. This was a very big deal. I remember my answer. I said to Artie, "Do you think I can do it?" He was characteristically Artie. He said, "Why the fuck would I have suggested it if I didn't think you could do it." Artie Miller agreed and Sullivan went along. I was made an Assistant Superintendent. Ronnie wasn't there.

This was a big promotion for me. I was in charge of everything that happened on that floor and I had to compete with the other assistant supers to get the sub's attention and do my work. So one thing that I would do was get in really early and visit the subs in their shanties, and tell them what I needed to be done. Almost every day I went to see the carpenter. I would walk into the shanty, which was just one of the guest rooms, and the guys would be in there changing and I just ignored them.

I never had a problem with any of the carpenters as I didn't have any problems with most of the men. The biggest problem was being humiliated in front of them, because they didn't know what to do and neither did I. That is part of the problem with sexual harassment. It affects everyone around. If a man wants to defend a woman who is being harassed, he will end up making himself a part of the problem, and he knows that. So, he does nothing, and then he gets angry at himself, and ultimately ends up blaming the woman and convincing himself that women don't belong on construction sites. Human nature. The abuser doesn't want women around, the guys who go along with him don't want women around and the guys who want to defend the women, ultimately don't want women around. What about the guys who don't give a shit? Good question. Not picking sides can be a viable position, but, not when the parties are not equal. Things are different now, and if a man sees another man abusing a woman or someone abusing a minority, the best thing to do is report it himself. Or he can talk to the abuser. Back in my day, there was no reporting. So the guys who didn't care probably had the right idea, in that they ended up doing the least harm.

Ronnie, the head super gave me my own laborer, Marcus. He was a magnificent looking bald Jamaican man and I loved him. He did whatever I asked. That got me into trouble sometimes, but it also got things done. One time I needed to have a hole made in the floor and it was work the plumber was claiming. So I told the plumber to do it and he blew me off. I tried for two days and said, "Fuck it." Marcus got a hold of a jackhammer and made the hole. There was a grievance filed against me by the Plumber's union and I was fined 2 days' pay at the full journeyman rate, but I got my hole.

Another time, I got into a fight with the ironworkers. We had this amazing glass light fixture paneled ceiling in the ballroom. The lights and the ceiling hung off a steel framework, but the point where the fixture itself was connected to the steel required a plate and a weld. Both the iron workers and the electricians claimed it, and in the meantime, nothing was getting done. So I directed the electricians to do the work. This time I was fined by the ironworkers, who quickly resolved their differences with the electricians and I got my ceiling built, and a fine.

I had an accident that I thought might ruin my career. The entire kitchen was full of stainless steel tables. The kitchen supplier who was a sub to the owner installed these and we were supposed to keep them protected. They were covered and no one was supposed to walk on them. They were installed before I was super, but I inherited them and got the job of cleaning them up. The coverings were missing in a lot of areas or worn out and the tables were in pretty bad shape. Ronnie came to me one day and said you have to clean up these tables tonight because the owner is going to come in tomorrow. I should have suspected something because the owner had people on the job and they were always there. Ronnie said to get Marcus to wipe them all down with Sure Clean. I didn't know what that was but I knew it was for cleaning and Marcus had it. So he cleaned all the tables and they looked great.

The next morning I went right to the kitchen and to my horror, all of the stainless steel tables were covered in rust. I almost fainted. I thought I would be fired for sure, but nothing came of it. The owner got someone in to grind the tables down and that was it. I never heard a word, I wasn't even teased about it. To this day I remember that sinking feeling. I have to admit that I think Ronnie set me up. But why would he take a chance like that? Sure clean is a bleach or an acid, probably used to clean stone or grout. Who knows? It must have been that the arrangements for the resurfacing had already been scheduled and Ronnie knew it. He fucked with my brain a lot.

I had another accident that almost ruined my life. The 5th floor was about 16 feet high. The Trumps wanted the Ballrooms to have a higher ceiling so we removed the part of the 6th floor above the Ballrooms and that added about 10 feet. There were very deep steel beams that divided the space into three. The beams could not be removed so the idea was to make them into a feature. We wrapped them with sheetrock and covered them with peach colored mirrors. Underneath, we created a pocket with a track where a moveable wall could run, so the room could be divided into three sections, for smaller groups. In the center of each of the three spaces was the fantastical glass lighted ceiling.

The concrete was removed in such a way as to leave a ledge encircling each of the spaces. This created a kind of catwalk where some mechanical equipment could be located. The ledges were rough but they would ultimately be hidden by the sheetrock encasing them.

Before I went to visit the subs in their shanties, I would check the work that was done the prior day so I could layout my own plans for what I needed done. This day I went up to the sixth floor and walked out on the catwalk ledge to look at the progress the electrician was making up there. It was just after 6:00AM. I made one misstep and I was off the ledge, stopped only by a single layer of sheetrock which was attached below. That went down and I grabbed on to the ledge. I pulled myself back up and ended up with only some scratched up arms and legs. That ledge was about 18 feet above the concrete floor below. Had I fallen, it would have been another hour until I was discovered.

I was definitely on the map now, as a super, and Ronnie was not thrilled. He was no champion of women on the job, he wouldn't hear of it. He didn't give me any direct shit but he loved reminding me of that. The higher up on the chain I got, the more subtle the harassment was. At the Hyatt, I heard a lot of the "what is wrong with you?" type but, see, it didn't bother me as much now because I had a better sense of myself. By the time I got to Trump Tower, that argument became absurd. Imagine someone saying what is wrong with you to a vice president of the Trump Organization? Of course, I didn't realize it at the time, but I was repressing my own desire to get pregnant because I knew that would have been the end of my career. But in the office, what I heard most was women can't be in the trades, in other words, they can be a superintendent or a Project Manager, that's easy work. They can't handle the work of a mechanic.

  I was not tormented in the office and I had my fellow assistant supers, Tim and Nino, who were incredibly supportive of me, so I wasn't alone. Artie, my mentor, was the very face of sexual harassment but he also didn't bother me because I had self-confidence, and no one took him seriously, least of all me, when he made sex jokes. Plus he spoke the same way to everyone and no doubt he was single handedly creating the most hostile of environments, but the women he came into contact with were mostly all of his own choosing, and we all told him to go fuck himself. I did have to slow dance with him at the company Christmas party and that was awkward. Yuck. But though Artie's behavior didn't bother me, the guys in the field still got under my skin and out there, I was really alone. I still continue to block some of this, but, through the writing process, I have recalled many things. I went to lunch a lot with sub's company bosses on all my jobs and many of them made me uncomfortable, asking me out when they knew I was married. And there were the body describers who told me what they thought of mine in front of all the other guys. My strength was real, but summoning it up constantly hardened me. I made real sacrifices and I will always be angry about that. I changed for the job. I learned about rage on the construction site.

Most victims of sexual harassment blame themselves. I was no different. When Hertenstein was torturing me, he was attacking my choices, my personality. That kind of attack made me feel like I was a bad person. It made me feel like I was a bad wife. Having this happen with other people around and no one defending me made me feel that I was unworthy of having friends, that I was not likeable.

The abuse at the Hyatt came after I felt I had found myself and I had confidence in having chosen to be an engineer. But the attacks as to my own sexuality made me feel like I was being provocative, or saying the wrong things – inviting the attacks. None of this is logical, especially if you saw the way I dressed on the Hyatt. I had jeans on and worked in an old Army jacket because the building was so cold. Everyone in the field worked with a coat on. Mostly I questioned everything about myself, and I internalized the abuse. It was much later when I confronted what happened to me, and how I handled it.

Having Ivana Trump around on the Hyatt and later, Trump Tower, was good and bad. She was certainly a woman of authority, on the one hand, but on the other hand the men looked at her as the pain in the ass boss's wife. That she was beautiful was a blessing and a curse. My own looks, though not on a par with Ivana's, opened and closed doors for me as well. I could get attention for myself that I might not have if I were unattractive. On the other hand, being attractive invited all the insinuations of sleeping around. Although I know of another woman in the field who was anything but attractive, and that didn't stop the men from saying she was sleeping with the boss. Probably some of the people who helped me also liked my looks. I guess in the final analysis it was neutral. However, Ivana was a sight to see and I think that helped her get her way more often. The fact that there was another woman now on the job made it better for me. As numbers of women increase, the effect of the harassment dampens and often the frequency. Plus they now have someone to talk to. At Trump Tower, Ivana was a force and nobody fucked with her, and this reinforced my authority.

I got into a few run-ins with Ivana at the Hyatt. Mostly we got along real well though and she liked me. We used to talk about this one young laborer who was often working on the roof with his shirt off. Imagine that. Ivana frequently commented to me about men. I got to know Ivana and Donald when I was a mechanical super because at Artie's direction, I attended the Owner's job meetings with the Architect and Engineer. I caught Donald's eye by accusing the architect of being full of shit. He was trying to blame HRH for a problem that was very obviously the architect's fault. I always spoke out at meetings. To me, respect didn't necessarily mean being quiet, although I later learned that some bosses do not want subordinates to be heard. I learned that the hard way. But, Donald and Artie both liked my honesty and fearlessness, and it served me well on the Hyatt and Trump Tower.

Ivana got very involved with the finishes toward the end of the Hyatt project. She had a decorator, also named Barbara, with whom she worked very closely and Barbara liked to give orders in the field. This was an absolute no no, and I handled it very easily. The first time she told a painter to change something, or to redo something, I took his change order over to her and insisted she sign it. She wouldn't. Then I got a hold of the painting foreman and brought him over to Barbara and introduced them although they knew each other well. I told the foreman if he did any work under her orders, he could expect not to be paid, unless she paid him herself, or got the owner to pay him. HRH would not pay for any work ordered by the decorator. (Or as Artie called them, desecrators). This worked with Barbara but was not so easy with Ivana.

She drove Nino crazier than me. Nino was the super on the bottom of the building where the Lobby and Restaurant were and he was a very experienced and seasoned Superintendent, who had done several buildings on his own. She would come in and order workers around. They would be doing something for Nino and she would stop them to do something else. She would change things on the spot, like grout colors. The trades loved it because it was the owner's wife and her word meant change order dollars. I tried the same trick with Ivana as I did with Barbara, but only when it came to the trades. I would never talk to Ivana that way, although I did ask her respectfully to go through proper channels. Trump had people on the job but they couldn't do anything with her either. The good thing was she didn't come around every day. If we didn't care about the job, we could have just gone along with whatever she wanted, and fixed it later. But it was our job to look after the project and do what was right for the project.

It was my experiences on Citicorp and the Hyatt job that shaped the approach I would take to work for my entire professional life. I am project oriented. I will do what is right for the project even if it means ruffling feathers with my bosses. Sometimes what is right for the project might not look like what is best for the company, like paying the subs on time and fairly. I knew that it was better to have the subs on your side and I would often take on my bosses to fight for a sub as I did with Bob Dexter at Citicorp. Mostly the choices I had to make were obvious and I got along. This has served me well, to say I work for the project, but it is heavily reliant on me being right most of the time, isn't it? Well, that is where the self-confidence comes in. Making a few wrong decisions and a lot of right ones is better than not making any decisions because you fear being wrong. Construction is not for the weak hearted.

Chapter 7 - Trump Tower - A Position of Respect

When the Hyatt Hotel was opened, we had a massive party in the Ballroom. My ballroom! There were a lot of political celebrities there like the mayor and big development people like Harry and Leona Helmsley. I remember thinking Leona was one of the most beautiful and elegant women I had ever seen and the Helmsleys were fantastic dancers. The room looked fabulous and the Trumps were in their glory. This was the watershed point in Donald's career. After the deal on the Hyatt, taking it from a blight on the city scape, through negotiating tax credits to make it attractive to Hyatt, getting special permits to do the work and then completing it, cemented Donald's position in the development world. And we all know, that was only the beginning.

I introduced my husband to Donald and Ivana at that party. Donald said to Pete, "Barbara is a terrific gal, she's going to work for me." Then Donald said to me make an appointment with Ivana to come over to the apartment. Then they danced together to the door and walked through. In 10 seconds my life had changed forever.

I knew the Trumps liked me a lot but I had no idea this was coming. I went to see Donald and Ivana at their apartment on Fifth Avenue, a few days later. We sat in the living room. I remember the breathtaking view of Central Park and that everything in the room was white – the furniture, the rug, the curtains. They had a built in bar and Ivana offered me some orange juice. All I could think of was a big orange stain on that rug. I declined.

Donald came right out with it. He said, "I want you to build Trump Tower for me." I had been preparing for this meeting with my husband Pete since that fateful night. I did not expect that he was going to put me in charge of the project, I hardly even knew anything about it. I was just expecting to be offered some job on it. Donald described the project to me. He said it was going to be 70 stories, with offices and luxurious shops, the most luxurious shops in the world, and then the top floors were going to be condominium apartments like Olympic Tower, only better. In his inimitable way, Donald informed me that I was about to be the person in charge of construction of the "most important project in the world."

Donald told me he and Ivana thought I was fantastic and it was first Ivana's idea to hire me. Every once in a while I remind myself that it was Ivana who got me there. Donald said that he thought that men worked better in business but a good woman is better than 10 men and I was that woman.

He meant that but I don't think in a sexist way. I think he was saying that most women don't have the stomach for the industry and that most of the men you ran into were blasé and ordinary. But a woman who had achieved something was invariably far superior to the men in her class. I know Donald was heavily influenced by his mother who worked hand in hand with his father in all the residential construction they had done over the years. Also Donald had a tremendous amount of faith and trust in Ivana. I later learned that he was also working with Louise Sunshine, a most powerful woman, who later became one of the movers and shakers in New York Real Estate. So I am giving Donald a pass on that comment. I will also say, and repeat later, that Donald, for all his womanizing and commentary, was the least sexist boss I ever had as far as trusting me and viewing me equally with all the men we encountered in our mutual dealings. I do not believe he ever made a comment behind my back about me being this way or that because I was a woman. And though he may have called me a bitch, I doubt if he used any of the other six words to describe me.

Donald told me he didn't have time to be so hands on anymore. He wanted me to be him on the job. He said I would be like a "Donna Trump" and I would treat everything as if it were my project, and my money, and I would be his final word. Although I realized, then and now, that he would never be hands off, I could see this was a vast amount of power and a very important and demanding job. Something I never thought about doing – way past my current level, or so I thought.

Donald told me he wanted me to start very soon and he would pay me $55,000/year. That was about 25K more than I was making at HRH. I don't remember how we left it. I guess he just assumed it was a done deal, but for my part, I was in total shock.

Pete and I were living in the city at the time, on 72nd Street on the East side. Pete was working in New Jersey for Ebasco Services and was already home when my meeting was over. I hopped in a cab. I told Pete "I can't do it," and he laughed at me. Pete has always been my biggest supporter. I said I wouldn't know where to start, who to talk to. He said people will seek me out and I will immediately take charge of everything that comes at me, because that is my nature. He was right.

There was one big problem, and that was Artie Nusbaum. When I told him I was going to work for Donald he was flabbergasted. He said it was the end of my career and that I was going to stop learning. Artie told me I was the best young assistant super he had ever worked with. He was going to bring me into the office and groom me for vice president. Hell, Donald was making me a vice-president on day one. Plus I knew the people in Artie's office and many of them were absolute snakes. One snake, in particular, who would be my direct competition. I also didn't have the same low opinion of Owner's Representatives as Artie did. (After working with me on Trump Tower and the Hartz Mountain job after that, I am sure Artie changed his mind about that subject.) Artie saw owner's reps as do nothing figure heads, usually architects. We universally agreed that architects belonged in the office and engineers in the field. And to a large extent, Owner's reps did not take over the job, they just decorated it. I had no intention of letting that happen on my watch. I may have not been sure I how I would handle it, but I was sure that it was going to be my project and I was going to be in charge. In a way, Artie's criticisms and his dismissal of the importance of the owner's representative only served to make me more resolute in my convictions. Nusbaum ran up against me several times on that project. Anyone who worked on Trump Tower knows I was in charge.

Artie really worked me over. Pete and I talked about this. As far as Pete was concerned it was a no brainer. But, I had an attachment to HRH and I was afraid to go out on a limb without a rabbi. (That means someone of high position to champion me.) Plus Trump already had people working for him and if he was willing to just dump them, what would he do with me? And for another thing, he treated them pretty badly. But on the other hand, they didn't stand up to him very well, and overall, no one at HRH had much respect for the Donald's people, fairly or unfairly. I decided it was too good an opportunity to pass up. I would make it work for me. Pete and I took a vacation cruise in Greece and I started as soon as we returned. September 1980. I had just turned 31.

One of the most remarkable things that happened when I started working on Trump Tower was the press attention I received. Everyone wanted to do a story about me. We agreed to let the New York Daily News do a feature about me as the first women to build a major skyscraper. Now, I never knew where all this attention came from but it had to be Donald. To this day, I can't say for sure I was the first woman to be in charge of a big building in a big city, but it is probably true and since the city was New York, my guess is I was the first woman engineer in the world to be in charge of the construction of a major building. Donald was the best promoter in the world. Somehow, I imagine he got out the word that he had hired a woman to build Trump Tower and it took off.

I was followed around by a reporter and a photographer for a day. I think we got editorial review, I am not sure, but I was very careful about what I said, anyway. I would learn the hard way about how to talk to reporters. But for this first encounter, I managed to get lucky and nothing that was printed caused me any problems. We spent time in my office and we went out to the field and met with the men, all the while I was doing my work. I changed my clothes and then changed them back. Every step of the way, the photographer was clicking.

The piece was set to run on December 9, 1980. On December 8, John Lennon was assassinated in front of his apartment building The Dakota, in New York City. My story did not run in New York, as it and many other features were abandoned to devote several of the paper's pages to covering Lennon's brilliant life and tragic death.

Of course, it was a tragedy for my career too. I was honestly extremely disappointed. I had been so excited about this publicity and Donald was looking forward to getting some free advertising. The story appeared in the Staten Island edition of the paper and one of the other boroughs, either Queens or Brooklyn, so some people saw it, but it was no great shakes. Surprisingly though, the story was picked up by the Associated Press which then resulted in my feature appearing in a diverse set of newspapers across the country with pictures. I remember hearing form people in St. Louis, Florida, New Orleans and California, Oregon. It was still being picked up a month later.

The press story gave rise to an invitation for me to appear on a television quiz show called *To Tell The Truth.* This show featured real people who had done something unusual that was interesting but not enough to make them familiar faces that could recognized by a panel of diverse mid-level celebrities. The kinds of people who made this show were people that did unusual jobs or had extreme experiences or accomplishments. Often, their names were known, but not their faces. The commentator would read a short biography and the camera would go to the three contestants and one would claim to be the subject. The real person and two imposters would answer questions from the panel and then the panel would decide who the real person was. The real person was forced to tell the truth in the answers whereas the others could just make things up.

The emcee read my bio – "My name is Barbara Res and I am a licensed engineer. I have worked for several construction companies and now I am in charge of the construction of Trump Tower. I am the first woman in the world to ever hold a position like this." Etc. etc. All the while he was talking, the camera focused on the three contestants and also on a 4 foot high scale model of Trump Tower. When he finished, each of the three of us stated, "My name is Barbara Res," and then took a seat.

My panel was composed of Nipsey Russell, the comedian, Polly Bergen, model and actress, Soupy Sales, comedian and TV personality and another actress. The panelists asked us various questions like one question I got, "what are pilings?" and I had to answer the truth so I explained pilings. But that was not the question that eventually gave me away. It was a question from Nipsey Russell who wanted to know which campus at CCNY the Engineering School was on and I had to say the North. So we only fooled three of the four so we only got $300 to share. It would have been $500 if we fooled all four. Imagine. That was the prize. Also I got an Odyssey which was an early computer game, and a 1 year supply of Borax products which turned out to be a hell of a lot of boraxo. But it was fun. Just so it doesn't seem so ridiculous, one of the people taping that day was the now famous writer and journalist, Letty Cottin Pogrebin. Besides, Rosa Parks was on this show too along with several other major personalities.

It helped me to be involved in the publicity because it increased my job security. But I don't think I ever needed that. Donald was an incredibly supportive boss, even if his reasons were suspect. Everyone who worked for him reflected back on him, so they all had to be the "best". The more public I became, the harder it would be for him to get rid of me because that would be like admitting I wasn't the best. But this is all speculative because I did a good job and Donald was good to me.

One of my first encounters with Donald was very important to our future relationship. He had torn down the old Bonwit Teller building and we were putting Trump Tower in its place. We had applied for a special tax abatement and the Department of Housing and Preservation was giving Trump a hard time. The head of the Department, Tony Gliedman, known to us through Donald as the "fat fuck," denied his application. Donald had to go through a lot of legal hurdles but he finally got the abatement which translated into millions of dollars for us. And, Donald ended up hiring Gliedman several years later for another job because Tony was a very savvy and politically connected lawyer. Donald always had a special disdain for overweight people, but a great eye for useful people. Donald never let prejudice come between him and a good deal.

One of the things Donald needed to do to get his abatement was to prove that the old building, which was now gone, had been functionally obsolete. He could do this by having an engineer certify this information. He knew I was a licensed professional engineer and asked me to do it. I said I couldn't because I never even saw the building. I probably said something like, "Are you nuts?" The point was that he was kind of pissed for a while but then realized that I had a certain kind of integrity that he could rely upon and manipulate as well. He got the engineer who did the demolition plans to make the certification. Anyone with a brain could tell you that a failing department store in a collapsing 5 story building on Fifth Avenue was functionally obsolete. The law was a stupid one, with enough loopholes that you could drive a truck through it. The "fat fuck" hated the idea that a luxury building like ours was going to get a big tax abatement, but he went about it all the wrong way. Nothing Donald did was inconsistent with the letter of the law and many luxury condos got the same tax breaks.

Donald NEVER asked me to do anything that wasn't 100% above board, mostly because in my dealings with him he was pretty much on the up and up, but also, Donald knew I would not do anything dishonest or illegal. Of course I bent the rules or played them like they are meant to be played. And that was good enough.

I worked in the office building at 730 Fifth Avenue, on the 2nd floor. It was called the Crown Building. Donald had the corner office. Next to him was Harvey Friedman, a lawyer and Real Estate guru. On the 57th Street side were two offices. One was empty, later to be occupied by Robert Trump, and the other one I used. Across from me were David Sklar, a rental agent, and in a much larger, nicely decorated office close to the entrance was Louise Sunshine.

I stayed in that office for about a year. I used to get in at 7:00AM and for a while, Donald used to beat me in. Then I think when he saw that I was willing to turn on the lights and answer the phone, he decided to come in a little later. And I did just that, I used to answer the phone until someone came in and I would be there at night too, so I got to hear some pretty interesting callers. I lived on 72nd Street and Third Avenue. There was a bus that stopped at the corner of Third, went up to Fifth and turned down Firth and stopped in front of the building. So it was a ten minute ride for me. Later, when I moved to New Jersey, it would be a bit tougher to get there much before 7.

When I started the project was in foundations, demolition had already been completed. Trump Tower was what is called a "fast-track" job, which means you start the work before the drawings are finished. One of my jobs was to make sure the drawings were getting done expeditiously and trying to avoid extra costs down the road because we started early without plans. HRH was the general contractor again, on a costs plus basis, and we had a budget and a schedule. We were going to try to do the job on a two day cycle. That means that we would work 6 days a week and complete 3 floors of concrete, once the project was in the full swing of things.

The building was 58 stories tall. The first 5 floors were very high because they were for retail, about 16 feet, then we had 11 stories of office space at 13 feet. There were three mechanical floors and then 38 stories of apartments at about 9 ½ feet. That makes the building over 650 feet tall. So if it had been only apartments, it would have been at least 68 stories.

Donald took the first 5 floors and called them Concourses. At the first of the office floors, which was actually the 6th floor, he relabeled it 16th Floor. The offices went up to 26th floor. The three mechanical floors brought it up to 29, therefore first apartment level was the 30th floor and the last, the 68th. That is how the building grew by 10 stories.

This was an all concrete building. We had a tiny amount of steel but all the main members were concrete. Donald said it was the tallest concrete building in the world. At the time, it was certainly one of the tallest, anyway.

When I started with Trump, I inherited an assistant who came from Bonwit Teller and had been involved in the demolition. His name was Tom. He was an OK guy but I don't think he expected to have someone come in and supervise him, and, for sure, not a woman. Tom was smart but not educated. Educated men were better dealing with me because there was no imbalance. Tom and I did not get along and it was very soon that Donald put him on other things and took him off Trump Tower.

The Hyatt was winding up and I was helping out with that by closing out subcontractors, negotiating their final contracts and approving their payments. Since Donald no longer needed the people at the Hyatt, he was letting them all go. But the one guy, who was the assistant, Jeff Walker, was to come and work for me. I was very happy about this because I always thought Jeff was terrific and suffered because his other boss did not stand up to Donald. I figured Jeff would work well with me and I was right. We also became best friends and we get together at least a few times a year.

Closing up the Hyatt and buying out Trump Tower at the same time worked in our favor because we were able to use some of the same contractors and take advantage of the volume. Leverage. But Donald had a secret weapon he used when we were finagling out the subs. Jeff and I would march them into Donald's office with the price we wanted in mind and if they started saber rattling Donald would pull a picture out of his desk and wave it in the air. "You wanna go up against this?" he would say. "I have him just waiting to sue you." The photograph was an 8' x 10' grainy black and white picture of Donald's friend, and personal lawyer, Roy Cohn. And he was scary enough in name without that photo. As a matter of fact, we did end up being sued by the electrician, and Roy took the case and I got to meet him. His office and his house were in a brownstone in the city. I never saw a more cluttered space in my life. This guy was a real character, and guess what? He really was scary. We settled that case in a month, and I never spoke with Roy again, but I saw him several times at functions. He and Donald were good friends.

I also hired an executive secretary, Roberta Bryant. Roberta was the most organized, bright and cheerful person I could have gotten. She was good looking too and had a wicked sense of humor. This team, with three additions, would be the best working group I was ever part of. My friend Jeff likes to joke that if we were on "The Apprentice" we would kick everyone's ass. No question, because for one thing, what we did day in and day out was real, and what we confronted was serious. Big money involved, and lives and real publicity. In truth, when I started with DJT in September, 1980, I was the real "Apprentice." We were inseparable. I learned from him, and he learned from me. We learned together. I would be surprised if Donald still didn't say that Trump Tower was his best job.

The planning for Trump Tower was endless. We were in fast track, so everything we did was done "now." For instance, we had an atrium with a full skylight which was to be like a beautiful garden, all marble and landscaping. There was a faceted marble wall, which water streamed over, and we called that the Waterwall. In the center of the Atrium, we would put tables and chairs. One of the special elements of the Atrium was the ficus trees. Our target opening was initially Fall, 1982, so in order for us to have trees ready, they needed to be selected and tagged right away, then followed up as they grew. Jeff was a tree expert on his own. I sent him to Florida with Tom Ballsley, our landscape architect, to hand pick the trees for the Atrium and the also the

Fifth Avenue Promenade. Then they went back to visit later to insure that the trees were being taken care of properly. We brought them up for installation early in the winter of 1983. In order to move the trees in to the space, we had to create a special heated pathway. It was all very tenuous because the trees were tropical and could not risk exposure to the cold, especially in the condition of being balled and away from the soil. The effort to move the trees in was herculean. There were four major ficus trees at the main entrance on Fifth Avenue and five trees in the atrium. The four were brought in through that specially created entrance on Fifth Avenue. The trees for the grade below had to be carried down in the truck elevator because they were so enormous they did not fit in the freight elevator. Then they were shuttled into the waterfall area.

Before we installed the trees, you could lean over the brass and glass railing and peer down to the atrium. Each floor was open to the atrium so you could see the entire waterwall, and all the marble planters and the marble floor from every level of the Retail portion and from the up and down escalators. It was just gorgeous. Then we started installing the trees. These trees were plainly magnificent. Jeff and Tom had done a great job with their selection and the trees were managed perfectly. Each tree had a location in the floor with a brass grate. One by one the trees were planted. When the job was done, the atrium looked like a tropical forest. The canopy of each of the five trees spanned about 20 feet. There was one big problem. You could not see the Atrium for the trees!

    The work was done on a Saturday and Sunday. Donald came in and saw the trees on Monday and he was horrified. The atrium was basically gone. All you could see were ficus leaves. One by one, he made us cut the trees down. It was surreal. These trees that had been nurtured for two years, and cost a small fortune to buy and move and install, we being chopped with a chainsaw. Jeff, Tom, the Architects, John Barie and Fanny Gong, the HRH Project manager, Aldo Rizzo and I, who had all been there when the trees were so gingerly put in place implored Donald to just remove two and leave the other three. Donald would not have it. With each tree we all rushed to see the various views of the Atrium. We told Donald you could see it now, and to leave the remaining ones. No way. We got to the very last tree. I remember standing at the railing with Donald. Augie, the labor foreman was down in the atrium with his chainsaw and Jeff and I literally begged Donald to save that one tree. I remember watching the blade enter the trunk and seeing the tree fall. It was an awful experience. But Donald was right. Maybe we could have left that one tree, but you really couldn't see the atrium with the original landscaping. It was a horrible waste of time and money but in the end, we had the planters full of other beautiful plants, and we installed smaller trees where the large ones were to be and the Atrium was truly a gorgeous focal point. But you will never see a space with such magnificent trees as the ones we cut down.

The trees in the promenade fared much better. They remained in their stately grandeur for a long time, welcoming the crowds who came in from Fifth Avenue. Of course, eventually what you were seeing was real trunks with fake leaves. Those babies shed like crazy. It was impossible to keep them healthy and to keep the floors safe and clean. Again, we gave in to the inevitable. (At some point, Donald made a deal with Gucci, and part of it involved redoing the entrance and the trees were eliminated. Even worse, the signature pink marble was replaced with black and white stone and the Marquee was re-designed along with the front of the building. Still a nice building, but Donald definitely gave away his signature, (or sold it, that is.)

Of course the trees weren't the only thing that had to be picked early. Everything at Trump Tower was an important design element and everything had to be pre-ordered. At the point in time when the foundation was just about done and the superstructure was beginning, not only had the plans not been finished, we had to still select all the finishes, the fixtures, the kitchens, the appliances and then evaluate them to see if there was money to be saved by changing things around.

It's hard to believe that we scrimped on things at Trump Tower, but Donald was all about saving, just as he had been at the Hyatt. Although everything was brass and marble, we didn't necessarily buy the best all the time. For example, the floors in the apartments were supposed to be wood. I had looked at Museum Tower, which was the closest new building that could even be considered competition and they had a herringbone wood floor with 3/4" pecan planks. Olympic Tower, arguably the most luxurious condominium at the time, had a plank floor as well. Donald wanted to go for a parquet which is also beautiful when done correctly, but he didn't want to spend the money. So we went with this 1/4" glue down oak flooring in one foot squares, the kind you would find in subsidized housing. Another place we cheaped it out was in the bathrooms. We purchased high end American Standard Plumbing fixtures, and then we used garbage marble. I was called marble 96 and was made out of an agglomerate of marble pieces and a matrix. We used the color Paradiso, which was the marble they had in Olympic Tower, but we went with the cheap stuff. Of course, Donald said it was the same as Olympic Tower. Louise Sunshine, who was in charge of selling the apartments, and I, fought Donald hard on this but he would not relent. Louise had also fought for a real wood floor. We ended up doing one foot square make believe marble tiles in the bathrooms, accompanied by cheap looking medicine cabinets to compliment the very expensive fixtures and faucets.

The kitchen cabinets were another joke. At the time, Pogghenpohl was the big name in cabinets and we wanted to copy them. We could have actually bought them but that was another story. We ended up with nice looking Formica cabinets that would have been just fine if you weren't buying a million dollar apartment. And the countertops, Formica again. By this time, Louise had given up. I was still fighting and Ivana was influential in getting certain things like post formed edges and touch up latches that made the cabinets appear custom made.

We also saved by going minimum code. In other words, although engineers like to build in extra capacity, we cut it all back so it just met the requirements of the City and National codes. By the way, the codes are more than sufficient. So we used the smallest pipes that were legal, and the fewest wires, etc. It turned out that this never caused a problem and in fact, unless you are planning an expansion, there is no need to exceed the codes when you are designing a building. However, I never argued with Irwin Cantor, the structural engineer, who was also known to overdesign. Trump Tower has to be one of the most solid buildings on earth.

Next thing was to attack each trade in the buyout. The first thing we bought was concrete. Donald, the man he was, was still afraid of his father. And truth be told, his father was still extremely influential on Donald because he supplied financing, and more importantly, had 40 years' experience in building concrete apartment buildings in Brooklyn and Queens. Fred Trump was a character out of Damon Runyan. He tooled around in a brown Cadillac limousine and had a brown logo and used brown ink in his typewriters. He also used plenty of brown dye in his otherwise grey hair. He was probably 75 when I met him and not active in building anymore, but he was as full of piss and vinegar as his son and wielded a giant stick. Fred forced his way into negotiations with the concrete contractors, against HRH's and my objections. Fred told Donald he wanted to pick the contractor, and that was that.

Let's say Fred didn't like me. It wasn't me, per se, it was the fact that I was female, 100%, Fred could not imagine a woman being in charge of the construction of any building, let alone the greatest of them all. So Fred didn't ignore me – I wish he had. No, he used me and aggravated me by constantly calling me, but gave me no credit or even acknowledgment. He gave me a ridiculous 1950's contract and insisted we use it to buy the concrete. HRH had already written the contract, and it was a good one. One thing HRH was great at was contracts. "No, No" Fred would say, "That's no good". A loud boisterous annoying big 75 year old was yelling at me because he didn't want to use the contract one of the major general contractors in New York was suggesting we use to buy millions of dollars' worth of concrete on an incredibly complex mixed use building the likes of which Fred had never seen. Yes, Fred drove me crazy. So, HRH and I had to pretend Fred was buying out the concrete contract. I would get yelled at, take the changes he wanted to make back to HRH and get laughed at. One way or another we got through it. Fred wanted to give the job to a friend of his, Dic Concrete, which we ultimately did. Unknown to us at the time was an alleged deal that the concrete contractors had made that this job was going to someone else. We had two very serious fires on the job while we were pouring concrete and the word is that Joe DePoala, the owner of Dic, was being punished for taking the job. For the time being, we gave him the job and everyone was happy, and Fred was passing out silver dollars. Fred had bought a few thousand silver dollars many years prior and used them as gifts or for celebratory purposes. So when we bought the job, about a dozen of us, HRH people, myself, the contractor's representatives got a sawbuck from Fred. It's kind of endearing but I would rather have just been left alone.

Fred was out of the job pretty soon after that, although he would insert himself every so often and it was always, "no, no, you can't do it like that". I can still hear that loud, impatient, "No, No, No". Donald told me that he had to reduce my reported salary to $49,000 because Fred wouldn't have me making more than his top person in his office, the Comptroller. Donald made up the $6,000 difference himself. Fred was really a piece of work.

Throughout the process, we would have parties, openings, etc. Fred was always there but he never ever gave me my props. It wasn't until Donald's wedding to Marla Maples, in 1993 that Fred, at 87, still with brown hair, came over to me and told me something to the effect that he knew he had always given me a hard time and realized that was wrong. He said it was because I was a female and he was very mad at Donald for putting me in charge. How could I possibly do the job - I was a woman and too young. He was used to the person Donald had working at the Hyatt, a fifty something year old man, and he wanted him to go to Trump Tower. Fred admitted he never gave me a chance and wanted me to know that he thought I did a really great job, and that I put up with a lot of crap, including from him. I guess you could call that an apology. So there's that – and the silver dollar.

The rest of the trades HRH and I bought out, with Donald coming in to make the final deal. Sometimes we made an arrangement in advance where we agreed to the absolute lowest number a sub could take and then we all went in to Donald with a higher price, so he could pull out the extra few bucks and look like a hero. A few times Donald did a lot better than we had and got a lower number.

Electrical was always my specialty so I attacked the drawings with a vengeance. I redesigned all the risers, eliminated feeders, eliminated panels, circuits etc. Then we gave my design to the contractors and told them make it work. It was a little too tight and they ended up having to do more work than I predicted. HRH had a contractor they wanted to give the job to who was allegedly "connected." I was opposed to this and we had another sub, Lord Electric, which was bidding lower. HRH did not know them and was pushing Garafalo Electric, its choice, very hard. We had a bit of a bidding war. Lord won the job at a very low price. HRH surmised that Lord was protecting a client interest. Equitable Insurance was Donald's partner in Trump Tower, and Lord did all of their work. For whatever reason, Lord was one of the larger contractors in NY, on a par with Fischbach, and knew what it was doing. Lord took the job. While we were bidding the electrical, I got a chance to negotiate with my old boss at Zwicker who was also trying to get the contract. By then, it was revenge enough to have him try to ingratiate himself to me after what had gone between us. If they had the right price, they would have gotten the job, no questions asked.

Lord took the job about $1,000,000 to low. Part of that was my fault pushing the redesign that didn't completely work, (for instance, I had not accounted for voltage loss over the very long feeders) and also Lord's ultra-competition to keep Equitable's work. About 3 months into the work I realized this and I spoke with HRH's people about it. I told them we need to make a contract adjustment. They told me I was absolutely crazy and do not under any circumstances say this to Donald. Lord is a big company, they can afford to take a hit. Plus there would be change orders. I kept my mouth shut. Lord would eventually default and need to be replaced at a cost to us of about $3 million. But HRH was right, Donald would never have gone along with my suggestion and it probably would not have made a difference.

It would have made a difference if we went with Garafalo though, because they went bankrupt in the middle of the job and left HRH stranded on several projects. The owner ended up going to jail for money laundering too.

We continued buying out trades. We gave some work to the guys we had at Citicorp and the Hyatt, and we took chances on some guys with really good prices like the plumber who never did a big project like this. One of the things I do not do my projects I learned at Trump Tower. I don't generally get performance bonds. If a sub defaults you call in the bond, but it takes forever the get the work started back up. You have to argue with the bond people as to what you are owed and you never get the real cost of the work back. Donald had me get proof from the subs that they had capacity to be bonded. That basically meant they were viable, and whatever the bond company would go after would be available to us. I am not sure that works anymore with everyone being corporately shielded but it is a good theory and bonds are incredibly expensive. Jimmy Whalen, the plumber, was capable of getting a $5 million bond and that was good enough for us. He turned out to be one of our best subs. I always told him I put him on the map.

When it came to appliances Louise and I had the same problems with Donald that we had with the finishes. We wanted to go with SubZero and Thermidor or Viking and Donald made us buy General Electric. But Donald was right about all of this too although, in a way, he was also very lucky. A lot of the people that bought apartments just bought the address. This was during the time that interest rates were crazy and a lot of Europeans were picking up pied a terres that they never even used. The finishes were good enough for them. But the majority of the people were doing their own thing, and they tore out most of what we put in, such as the marble in the bathroom and the parquet floors. In the tiny kitchens, people just left things alone. Maybe they would put in granite countertops and change the tile floor. But where there were big kitchens, everything came out and it would not have mattered what we put in there. We also had a lot of people combining apartments and in that case, the walls went too.

Probably the most important thing we bought on the job would be the lobby marble because that was the single identifier of the Trump Tower Atrium. All the effort, time and money that went in to buying the marble was worth it.

The architect brought us lots of samples for the marble in the lower floors. We finally decided on a pink/salmon color called breccia pernice. This would cover all the floors and walls on the retail levels and of course on the main entrance on Fifth Avenue. One of the zoning variances Donald got to allow him to put extra floors on the building was called a "through block" arcade, which means you provide a way for people to cross through your building, from one street to another. This is considered a public amenity and the city rewards developers for providing it by increasing the allowable square footage. There were other zoning bonuses, such as the ones for building parks, improving subways etc.

Our building entrance was on 5th Ave just next to Tiffany. However, we connected to the through block arcade at the IBM building to the West thereby enabling people to enter on 5th and leave on Madison or 56th street. When Bonwit Teller was re-built, we connected through that building to 57th Street. So our "lobby" was more of a thoroughfare, and truly luxurious one - all marble, bronze, tinted glass. And the marble was coral/pink.

Marble is a natural material and because of that it is rarely homogenous. The harder the marble is, the more likely it is a solid color so you can be pretty sure that every piece will look the same. That's why granites are so true. You buy one piece, it looks like another. With breccia marbles there are lots of different colors or hues of colors and varying veins of different colors and widths. This is what makes it most beautiful. But for this reason, no two pieces are alike. The same quarry that produces a stone of a basic color will produce an entirely different looking stone a year later.

So it was decided that we should go to Italy make sure that this was the marble we wanted and that there was enough in the quarry to insure we could complete the job. My memory says there was about 100,000 sq. feet of marble in Trump Tower. The walls were supposed to be the lighter version and the floors and waterwall, "scuro" which is the same stone but from a different part of the quarry. Once Donald saw enough of the stone, he knew he wanted it all to be the darker rich salmon color.

Chapter 8 - Construction Manager to the Stars

Donald could not come to Italy but five months pregnant Ivana came along with the marble contractor, the architect, John Peter Barie, and some people from HRH. We flew into England and then Rome and took a hop to Pisa. The actual quarry was in Verona but we were going to Carrera where the fabrication is done.

One of my most striking memories was waking up on the plane in the morning. I was ready to crawl into a hole. Ivana looked like she just stepped out of a salon. We had to do a lot or traveling yet before we got to Carrera. London to Rome, Rome to Pisa, then a drive. What practically knocked me out seemed to have no effect on her. I guess that's what all those years as a model did for her. She arrived in Carrera as fresh as a daisy.

We stayed in a hotel that was picturesque, it had mosquito netting on the beds! The owners of the plant that cuts the blocks of marble and processes it were feting us. We went to dinner in the mountains. It was the very first time I had seen a Portobello mushroom. They were served with shaved Parmesan cheese. It was also the very first time I had grappa.

The next day we went to see the marble. I remember Ivana looking at a huge slab and picking out a 6" square piece and saying that she wanted all the marble to look like that one section. It was impossible to convince her that the marble was non homogeneous and also that it would look bland if it was all just like that small piece. On the other hand, the marble slabs we saw were all over the place. Some were almost solid with heavy veins. Others were all patterned with light greens and yellows mixed in with the pink.

It was decided that we would get a large enough sample of the stone to bring back to the US and show Donald how it could be blended to make it work in is distinctive state. He ultimately approved the stone, but, as it turned out, the marble was so different by the time we got to the third floor, it looked like a different species, but it was so gorgeous, that it didn't matter. We could have just trusted the contractor. But then, I wouldn't have had my two trips to Italy. I have a remnant from the mockup that we brought back. It is about 5' x 4' and I keep thinking I should make a table of something with it. Truth is, the marble no longer exists in its natural state.

The tour of the factory was fascinating. We saw how marble was cut and polished. We saw how they do the flaming on granite to make it rough looking and we saw hundreds of stones in incredible shapes. There were carved pieces of furniture including whole bathtubs. At the time, more than half of the factory was tied up with projects in the Middle Eastern countries.

One memorable thing about Carrera was that there was marble everywhere. It was in the street like we have concrete pavement. All different shapes and designs. You could look at a house and know that marble mason lived there by the materials he used and the level of workmanship. It was very beautiful.

After the factory, we went to the Carrera quarry and learned how marble stone is taken out of the mountains. They drill and blast and pull out the stone in massive blocks. Carrera is a very familiar stone, mostly white with grey and black veins. You see it a lot in public toilets in the old buildings that were built at a time when public buildings were the monuments we now revere. It was a lovely trip.

One of the reasons Ivana wanted to come along was the fashion shows were going on in Paris a few days later. I stayed with her until she got to Paris. After we were finished in Carrera, she rented a Fiat and we drove up the autostrada to Bologna then the Italian Riviera and finally Monte Carlo, which is where we stayed. We really bonded on that trip. Ivana told me all about her life and working as a model in Canada, meeting and marrying Donald and their life together. Ivana was meeting up with a friend in Monte Carlo, Verina Hixon, who would eventually buy multiple apartments in Trump Tower and put a swimming pool in her living room. Verina was supposed to get us two rooms but Monte Carlo was extremely crowded and she could only get one. So I and the pregnant (with Ivanka) Ivana spent the night together in a double room in the Hotel de Paris in Monte Carlo. What an incredible place. It is opposite the casino on a huge square.

Verina made arrangements for our entertainment. I was amazed that I was included in the festivities, but she had always been very nice to me; she respected me. I worked very closely with Verina on her apartment in Trump Tower, until she eventually tried to bribe me. More on that later.

A man and his wife, friends, or acquaintances of Verina's is more accurate, picked us up at the hotel and drove us up into the mountains to a little town where we met a big crowd of other people at an out of the way restaurant. It was the first time I ever rode in a Rolls Royce. Some of the people were players and the others were wannabes. The founder of the feast was trying real hard to impress, but the main course of the meal was only pasta. But there was loads of flowing wine, salad fruit and dessert. Oh, Italy was where I learned to eat salad after the meal. At the dinner, I participated in the conversation as if I belonged. Ivana explained that I was in charge of construction of Trump Tower and everyone was very interested in me and the work I was doing.

When we were finished Ivana, Verina and I went with the couple that brought us to the Casino. This couple was what I call idle rich. They were incredibly wealthy with family money. Although the man claimed to work, I was pretty sure the only job he did was counting the cash. As I recall he was in jewels or stones of some sort.

The streets around the Casino were packed; you could hardly drive with the people on the street. At one point, the owner of the car, who was driving, made this simple statement as if he were reporting the weather. "They should let me take my rifle and shoot these pests. They should not be allowed to be here. They are only in the way." That was a rude awakening for me, I had never heard anyone talk like this. It actually scared me a bit. I was sitting in the back, wedged between Ivana and Verina and felt for the first time that I really did not belong. The man was very much in earnest, and I realized there are people in this world who truly believe they are better.

The casino was great, although I didn't gamble. First off, everything was in French and I couldn't even follow what they were doing. I just knew a lot of money was on the tables. There was a lot of champagne. Really rich people were playing Baccarat, no one I was with though. They just floated around chatting with people like them and laughing. It was like a scene from a Fellini movie.

We got tired and decided to leave early. Plus Ivana needed her sleep. Mrs. rich guy wanted to stay, so he very politely offered to drive us home. As the three of us, Ivana, Verina and I were about to climb in the back seat, he pointed at me and said, "You, get in front." It was obvious that he was concerned that driving alone in the front of the car with three women in the back would make him look like a chauffeur, god forbid. So he literally ordered me into the front. Working on Trump Tower would expose me to the many sides of wealthy and famous people and some of them are very ugly indeed.

We flew up to Paris together and Ivana stayed for the shows, while I took the Concorde home. That was interesting too. The plane was not nearly as nice as you would expect, but the waiting lounge was amazing. So was the food on the plane. But the very best thing was getting on the plane at 11:00AM in Paris and arriving in NY at 9:30. I took the Concorde again when I was looking at granites in Spain for Hartz Mountain. The Concorde no longer flies, and I personally blame misdirected environmentalists in the USA for the fact that airline travel is no better now than it was in 1969 the first time I flew on a plane.

We did things at Trump Tower that weren't done before and couldn't be done afterwards. While we were building, there was a massive fire at the MGM Grand Hotel in Las Vegas. As a result 6 story open spaces like our Atrium became a thing of the past. That fire had a tremendous impact on how buildings are built now in the city and even we made certain modifications to our systems to make the building safer, although we had followed all the codes already.

There was a collapse of a walkway at a Hyatt Hotel which was similar to a walkway we were building and that caused a lot of soul searching and recalculating. But our bridge was designed and built properly and it is still there, sturdy as ever. The business of Construction is a work in progress and the rules change every time something new is learned. Unfortunately it often takes a catastrophe to bring things to light, such as the recent crane accidents in New York that changed crane inspection and site safety on the job.

The way we kept our atrium safe from fire was to install a water curtain which is comprised of lines of closely spaced sprinklers which, if activated, would actually create a wall of water dividing off the atrium on each floor from the space surrounding it. However, 6 story atriums are now a thing of the past.

The worst incidents in terms of property damage we had at Trump Tower were fires during the construction phase and they were not accidents at all. When we were pouring concrete, there were two fires and both were ruled as Arson. The first occurred during the evening hours in November 1981. Donald and Ivana were at a Charity Dinner at the Waldorf. I was there too. We got word that the building was on fire. I remember going over there and seeing the flames. The fire department took care of it fairly easily and in terms of New York fires, it was not major. But you wouldn't get that from the press coverage. That was a black day, but not the blackest. The bulk of the damage for that fire was the destruction of the emergency generator. Because we had already paid for it, it was the owner's property; but it was covered under the builder's risk policy. As far as time is concerned, we pretty much worked around it and didn't lose but a few days. So other than the bad publicity, the fire did not hurt us too much. The second fire was a disaster and almost deadly.

At 5:30 AM on January 29, 1982, the phone rang, at home. I was already up getting ready to leave for work. It was Ivana. "The building is on fire, come here immediately." I rushed through and got out. On the way down, I heard it on the radio. When I got there, they were fire trucks all over, but the fire was out. They were working on getting the crane operator, Tommy Bracken, out of the cab of the tower crane. Happily, they did this without any injuries. An hour or so later, there would have been 100 or more men on the floor. The cause of the fire was arson. I do not believe this was ever resolved, or even properly investigated, but the rumor on the street was that Dic Concrete was being punished for taking the project. I guess the owner of the company didn't have the heart to tell Fred it was someone else's turn, or maybe he was just too greedy. But he paid the price. Whatever the reason, if Bracken had gotten killed, it would have been a homicide. This is the type of people we were dealing with and from whom I know HRH protected me. Trump Tower was Dic Concrete's last job.

During the fire, the 28th floor had partially collapsed. Several other floors were damaged by the fire and the water. The city and our own structural engineers were all over this because they wanted to make sure to devise a repair program that would insure that the building meets all safety standards. Donald of course wanted the work done right, but also, right away. He did not want to lose a moment he didn't have to. Plus, he was dealing with a nasty NY press that referred to the fire as the "Towering Inferno", and called the building jinxed.

We ended up removing the top two floors and reinforcing the concrete for several floors below. The expense was in the several millions and we lost at least two months to our schedule. We did, however, have a brilliant public adjustor and he made sure we got every cent of insurance, in spades. As always, the fire did not hurt Donald. If anything, he spun the publicity to his favor.

Of course, the marble was the most important finish of the atrium, but the most important structural design element was the ability to create so vast an open space without any columns. We accomplished with a space frame. The space frame is a set of interlocking structural members like trusses that are capable of carrying load over vast expanses. Our space frame came from France and was state of the art in 1981. Because it was a structural element it was made of steel. The finish on the steel was polished bronze. Once the space frame was erected, we installed a skylight over it to create the airy open look of the atrium, however, it was the space frame that carried the weight of the skylight and the potential snow load that it may handle from time to time. Most people don't realize that roofs are designed primarily to accommodate the load imposed by a heavy accumulation of snow.

Having the structure designed by Irwin Cantor and the space frame designed by Lev Zetlin, I can confidently say that Atrium is one of the safest places in New York. However, building it was extraordinary difficult. HRH made a mistake when it purchased the materials and that mistake was going to cost us about $20,000. Instead of just owning to it, one of the soldiers in the HRH estimating department came in to see me and Donald with the VP of the space frame supplier. They told us for an extra $20,000, they could get the finish upgraded to a shinier bronze. You can't say much better to Donald than the word shinier, so he agreed to the payment. I was a bit leery. I waited until that thing was going up and then I pulled out the original sample piece the contractor had brought in to show us when he was pitching the job. Looked the same to me, so I didn't pay the extra. I later learned what the reason behind the extra money was HRH had made a mistake in preparing the scope of the work and there was a legitimate extra. But I did not agree to pay it, under any circumstances. I have a hard time with liars, and if HRH had just said they made the error, I would have cleared it. Besides, that contractor made more money on advertising, using pictures of Trump Tower in his brochures, to pay for that change order 20 times over.

Having gone through the horrors of the fire and the rigors of the repair, the rest of the concrete work seemed like a breeze. We quickly got back on to the two day cycle and finished thirty floors in little more than 2 months. On a construction project, when the last floor is poured, or the last piece of steel is set, the building is considered to be topped out. It is traditional to raise a flag at the highest point and then to have a party. If it is an important project, you have a big party. For the Trump Tower Topping Out, the party had to be, of course, the best topping out party in the world.

The preparations were legion. We had a consultant named Mel Fante. The best word to describe him would be impresario, because party planner would imply nothing like the extent of the talents he possessed. Back then people released balloons, so we had 10 thousand balloons. The party favors were black cups and black ashtrays with the name Trump Tower and the date emblazoned in gold. Plus we had T-shirts in black and gold and also hardhats to match.

The Topping Out Party was held on July 26, 1982. We must have had at least a thousand people at the thing, because workers alone were over 500 and all the workers were there. The usual fare for a topping out party is big heroes with jug wines and beer. At Trump Tower, we had really fancy food, with champagne and a real bar. The trade's workers attended the party during their lunch breaks and then went back to work, but there wasn't much work done that afternoon. I remember Trump complaining that the workforce was being invited to the party but when he was reminded that the party was actually for them he relented.

I am not sure why, with all the construction going on at the time, that our building was the one which the mayor *and* the Governor felt not only appropriate, but necessary, to attend, but there they were there with speeches at the ready. True to the Luck of the Donald, while topping out parties don't get much coverage in the press, this one did. Mayor Koch was speeding in his limo to make it on time, and the car got into a fender bender with a local driver. Koch got rescued by a patrol car and shuttled to Trump Tower, sirens blaring. This story was picked up by the wire services and ran all over the country. Enough free publicity to pay for a lot of champagne.

Trump was always extremely well connected in terms of politics. This is something he inherited from his father who was part of the Brooklyn Democratic machine when there were machines. I, myself, strong armed a lot of subcontractors for contributions, mostly for really nice fundraising parties that were networking events that everyone enjoyed. The ones I remember most were Koch and Andrew Stein. Donald, too, was a Democrat back then and we had the borough president and half the city council there at the party as well as the Mayor. And of course, Hugh Carey. Governor Carey came to the party with his wife. In his speech, he singled out "the great NYC construction workers who fill our city's empty space with glittering towers of glass and steel," to thundering applause. Evangeline Gouletas Carey was the Governor's wife. She also was a celebrity on her own because she practically invented the practice of turning ordinary underutilized commercial buildings into luxury condominium conversions for tons of money. She took the microphone and directed the audience to give a round of applause to *me*, a woman she described as doing the same job that she did on so many projects. Of course, she wasn't an engineer and I wasn't a millionaire, but we both had brown hair.

The party was a great success and made the workers feel even more connected to the building. The fact that Donald was around the jobsite a lot, as well as Ivana, was very good for Trump Tower. Both of them acknowledged the workers and treated them with respect, and the Trumps were well respected in return. For myself, I practically knew every guy on the job. Of course that didn't prevent the few assholes from drawing pictures of Ivana and me, or writing poetry about us on the walls in the stairwells, but now I had a different way to handle this. I told HRH to paint it over whenever it cropped up. No one said anything, it just got painted over. My approach was the approach of someone in power. I could have sought out who did it, but instead, I made them irrelevant. No one would see their work because it was erased as soon as it was done, and what were they to do, complain. "Leave my graffiti intact.?" In one of life's great ironies, it has turned out that a quiet censure was better than a public trial. The message is, "you are not important enough to me, to single you out." I have the power to make you disappear." I am sure that the final result was the men ended up seeing these artists and poets as jerks. Unfortunately, while attacking me and Ivana made some guys into jerks, attacking other women did not meet the same scorn. We had the usual banquette of oglers and whistlers as any other site. Just like on the Hyatt. One guy alone may be fine. A group is another story.

We had a soft opening with Loewe, Charles Jourdan and Buccelatti's stores in November because they all had front doors on 5th Avenue and didn't need access to the atrium to operate. But the Grand Opening, at least the first of the Grand Openings was planned for Valentine's Day in 1983. From November on, we were geared up to getting as many stores as we could by this date and the complete Atrium and all the finishes up to the 3rd floor done.

Chapter 9 - The World Meets Trump Tower

At around 4:00PM on Friday, February 11, 1983, a film crew from ABC came into the Atrium to make a record of our progress for broadcast on the evening news. They filmed the atrium, still filled with scaffolds, the stores empty of stock without finishes in them, and a building that looked like opening was some months away. Snow had started falling and it was accumulating fast. It was clear that if we had been hoping to move materials into the building, it would now be next to impossible. So when I told the reporter who was shoving a mike in my face that we were on schedule to open that Monday she actually laughed at me.

Truth is, the reporter was clueless as to what was going on and had no inkling of just how precarious our situation was. What she thought were major problems were mere trivialities compared with the reality of what we had to deal with. We knew we would be working around the clock for the weekend, so Jeff and I had planned to stay at Donald's hotel on 59th Street, the Barbizon Plaza. Norma, Donald's personal assistant was going to stay with us and we had an out of town guest, a man from England who had made and overseen the delivery of the uniforms for the Doormen. Those uniforms became quite famous and the doormen too because they were captured tens of thousands of tourist's pictures. They wore bearskins which are these enormous fur hats that are the same as the Queen of England's guard's wear. The haberdasher who made our hats had worked for the royal family. They cost thousands of dollars. Along with the red woolen uniforms, our doormen decorated Fifth Avenue and went beautifully with the polished bronze marquee overhead.

The four of us planned to have dinner that night. When we finally headed up to 6th Avenue we were already trudging through a foot of snow. Because of the snow, and the fact that it was a Friday, and that our Waterwall was nowhere near finished, we were not the only guests at the Barbizon Plaza that weekend. HRH and I had decided that if we had any hope of seeing marble workers on Saturday, we would have to put them up too. So the entire crew of stone masons stayed in and ordered room service, including Dom Perignon, which we backcharged to the marble contractor. The food is one thing, but enough is enough.

Not only did we need masons, we also needed carpenters, electricians, plumbers, laborers, and every other mechanic and the word was out that we were paying overtime and double time on Sunday. We only had to put up the marble guys because they were super specialists and irreplaceable. For the most part, the rest of the people just needed to be skilled labor, not even, because surprisingly over the next days, Jeff, John and I would be doing all sorts of work that normally would have gotten us into big trouble with the unions, but anything went that weekend.

One of the big problems was that the stores weren't ready. There was a men's boutique on the

3rd Floor, called Napoleon, that couldn't open because it wasn't painted and had no floor. Given that, there were also no $3,000 Sport coats or $100 ties either. I told the owner to get the stock ready to come in on Sunday. He said I was crazy. But I had enough painters standing by to paint the coliseum. We put 2 coats of Navaho White on the walls, hung a few wood doors on the dressing rooms and were set to go. Except for the concrete floor. The design called for a custom carpet that was ready, but could not be delivered because of the snow. This was true for other stores as well. We had already sustained a good 12" of snow with no end in sight. I got hold of one of the laborers, who had a pickup truck. I told him to go out to this cheapo carpet place in Paramus NJ that sells carpet off the rolls. "Get all the beige carpet they have available." He came back three hours later with several hundred yards of imitation wool plush, and inexpensive Berbers. We put that carpet everywhere there were bare floors. In most cases, as with *Lina Lee*, the Rodeo Drive clothier, the floors were specially designed wood or some other material. While most of this work was done, whatever concrete floor remained uncovered got "Carpetland's" best. The men's shop owner transported his goods on Sunday through the now plowed streets from Third Ave and had them there for the opening. *Napoleon* was ready for business.

A very major problem was the waterwall. Unlike the floors which were still unfinished, there were no gaps in the waterwall, it was just that much of the marble was only hanging there, safely anchored, but not properly sealed. We just didn't have enough people and we were not ready. You could not possibly turn the water on without flooding the basement completely and knocking the building out. Plus, the water was going behind the wall, so there wouldn't be much of a "falling effect", that you could see anyway. Undeterred Jeff, John and HRH came up with a plan. The idea was to make it possible to get the waterfall operational for a short time, just enough time for Donald to make a speech, take the pictures, hear the oohs and ahhs and then shut it down for a month and finish it.

I am not sure how this happened because we were all going in different directions and I was concentrating on the retail, but John and Jeff ended up on the scaffolding stuffing pieces of carpet padding behind the curtainwall to seal off the openings. They kept talking about a weir. I didn't know what a weir was but it was god damned important and they needed to find a way to direct the water to the weir. They were using pieces of cardboard and metal and aluminum foil. But they pulled it off. The water went exactly where it was directed to go on the outside of the wall. And it looked gorgeous. No one could imagine it was just spit and glue. I was on the platform with Donald who was giving his speech. Jeff was at the base of the waterfall with walkie talkie in hand waiting for the speech to end. John was at the disconnect switch ready to turn off the water as soon as he was given the sign. Jeff was trying to give Donald the cut sign to end his speech, but Donald just kept going on and on. All of us were envisioning carpet padding flying across the atrium at any minute. Fortunately we made it. The water was shut off in time, but even with the water off, it was just as beautiful with the glorious salmon marble everywhere and the sumptuous landscaping. Not to mention those million dollar stores.

Donald and Joan miraculously got the finest jewelers in the world, *Cartier* and *Harry Winston* among them, to open satellites in the Atrium. At the party, I could be seen wearing a $50,000 diamond and ruby necklace from a jeweler called *Falconer*. This was owned by a Chinese man who brought us dim sum during the snowstorm crush. Of course, we had *Loewe* and *Jourdan* in full swing, with their incredible leathers, and *Asprey* which made china for the Queen.

There was a restaurateur who had opened not only a terrific Italian Restaurant next to the atrium, but had put a bar alongside the escalators and people could carry coffee and gelato to the tables and chairs under the waterwall. The owner of these two eateries was Dino De Laurentis, the director. He called the restaurant *DDL*. We also had a tiny confectionary right in front of the Atrium that sold super expensive and super delicious chocolates. I believe they made the thousands of chocolate hearts wrapped in gold foil that were ubiquitous in the Atrium that day.

After the opening, we went back to the work of finishing the project. The next big target was bringing in office tenants and we had some heavy hitters there as well. One of the tenants was the owner of *Candies*, the Shoe People. They had a major opening party planned for the Atrium in June. That same month, we also were hosting a Party for *New York Magazine* with a few thousand people. These parties were great fun. There were always lots of glittering people, often celebs. Getting the office done was important but it was a relative non-event after the trouble we went through to get the first retail done.

On April 4, 1983, Paul Goldberger, the Architectural Critic for the New York Times wrote his review of Trump Tower. It was glowing. I always wondered if the fact that when he came to visit the construction site, I had Spielberg there, and Goldberger was more excited about meeting Steven than anything else, influenced him to write a favorable review. Here is a direct quote: "The atrium of Trump Tower may well be the most pleasant interior public space to be completed in New York in some years. It is warm, luxurious and even exhilarating." One of the things Paul liked best about the Atrium was the way the stone cladding on the columns made them round and soft - "absolutely sensuous". Those corners were the source of a major fight between Donald and the architects, and of course, ultimately they became my problem.

Everyone knew that the marble was 3/4" thick on the walls. This was the appropriate size to use, so it was substantive and not merely a veneer. But everywhere you could see the dimension of the marble, Donald wanted it to appear as thick as possible. So in some places, such as the waterwall, pieces were 1-1/4". On the columns the marble faces were applied to overlap. There are several ways you can apply stone to a column. Besides overlapping, you can miter the joint, or to make a quirk miter that squares off at the very end of the joint. This marble was too vulnerable to miter. It would break off, and the quirk miter, which probably would not have worked anyway, looked like crap. Donald was beside himself. He told me the columns ruined the atrium, made him look cheap, made the marble look cheap etc. Initially, the architects got the brunt of this, especially Fanny Gong, who is a superb architect and human being, and was the unsung hero of the public space design, but it was I who was supposed to ultimately solve the problem and since there was no solution, I got slammed too. Donald came up with an idea. He wanted us to make bronze covers to attach to the 4 corners of each column. I don't remember if we mocked this up, we certainly drew it and everyone thought it looked awful. Donald told me to do it. I didn't. I think he knew I wouldn't do it, and when I finally came back to him to tell him it was very expensive, he had gotten over it and let it go. When I saw that Goldberger review, I was all over Donald. He was too happy with the review to realize I was being insubordinate.

Besides the office section, we also had the rest of the stores to finish up and the 4th and 5th floors to open. Then there was the left over patch jobs that had to be rectified. *Lina Lee* was a very special store, right from the start. It was one of the sparks that ignited the excitement about our retail, carefully nurtured and calculated by Joan Siegel, a retail specialist Donald hired, and paid a small fortune to, to market us throughout Europe. It was she who captured Loewe, a Spanish leather retailer which opened its very first store in the United States right here at the South East corner of 5th and 58th. Next to Loewe was Charles Jourdan, who was snatched from their other 5th Ave location to the Trump allure. Both Jourdan and Loewe had 3 story spaces. Asprey of London was another main level tenant, known for its fine jewelry and statuary, but best known to Americans as the creators of the Heart of the Ocean worn by Kate Winslet in Titanic. Also on the First at 58th Street was *Cartier*. In a jewel box of a kiosk on the 2nd Floor overlooking the main entrance was a pink marble *Harry Winston*. But the most exciting and dynamic store we had was *Lina Lee*.

I think she may have come from Texas or somewhere in the South, but Joan found her on Rodeo Drive and she was the hottest thing on the street. She sold clothes designed for her own label, made of the finest silks, wools and leathers. Her clientele in Los Angeles was a virtual who's who and she was expected to bring them to Trump Tower. On that she delivered.

Although we got the highest prices ever paid for retail space inside a building, and on the street, we still managed to sock these guys with big charges for tenant finishes, courtesy of fine print in the leases and my careful reading of same. For instance, the tenants were required to pay for their storefronts. We charged Jourdan $500,000.00 for the marble and bronze that ran along its demising wall separating the back of store from the main entrance to our building, and they paid it. It's so ironic because the day Jeff and I went to negotiate with their executives, I passed Bergdorf Goodman and in its window on 5th Avenue was a *Charles Jourdan* display. I told Joe, the exec we were negotiating with, that not only did I want the $500,000 but I wanted those blue pumps in Bergdorf's window in an 8B. I got the shoes the next day. The cash took a bit longer.

Perks like that were common place at Trump Tower. *Lina Lee* and her husband Allen Lidow took a liking to me when we first met to go over their plans. Obviously, I had to approve anything that was done inside the building, and I had to coordinate the systems with our contractors. Lina had an architect who was pure LA. He was really a designer who did surreal tile work for movie stars in LA and his claim to fame was an Oscar for a documentary. We needed to meet periodically so Allen and Lina asked me to come out to LA to take a meeting with their whole crew. They flew me there first class, (I would have done that anyway), had me met by a white stretch limo and put me up at the Beverly Hills Hotel. The next night I had dinner at their house in Bel Air and the following day we met at their store on Rodeo. Lina told me to take anything I wanted, she would give me 50% off. That was an offer, I could resist because a blouse in that store was $500.00. But the trip was a romp, I got to hold a real Oscar and meet some characters at that famous bar in the Beverly Hills Hotel.

    I helped the Lidows a lot with their store and navigated the waters with the contractors and the unions. Working with me and an assistant project manager at HRH, *Lina Lee* had a very successful opening on Valentine's Day. As a thank you she gave me a $2,000 gift certificate and $1,000 to the project manager to shop at the store. Before I took this offer, I cleared it with Donald, who said go for it. By the time I was finished I had spent $3700, on a wool jacket and slacks, a blouse, a leather skirt, a suede top and a belt. So I spent $1,700 of my own money on top of the gift certificate and was lucky to get out of there without buying more. Talk about the pressure sell. But the stuff was gorgeous. On the days I wore Lina, I dressed like a movie star!

    I did Allen Lidow a really big favor later on so if he hadn't gotten his money's worth already, he certainly did now. *Lina Lee* took more space and did an expansion less than 2 months after they opened which involved a lot of carpentry work. Lidow wanted to use his shop dressers from Los Angeles. I told him no way and he ignored me, and brought these guys in over a weekend. Worse than that, even, the trucks that delivered the fixtures were nonunion. So I had the teamster and carpenter shop steward to deal with. Lidow was an arrogant prick. He went back at them with barrels blazing, told them to fuck off and I was left with the carnage. I remember standing in the lobby in front of the elevator at around 9:00 at night arguing with the Teamster, him stepping on to the escalator and his words, "Lidow is dead."

I cannot say if I saved the man's life or only his legs but I managed to broker a deal that enabled Lidow to use his people through a special arrangement with the carpenters union known as a job shop agreement. There was another "special" deal with the two stewards, the details of which I will never know. HRH was most influential in the success of this endeavor, but all behind the scenes. From my vantage point, it was just the two stewards, Lidow and me. Lidow turned out to be a real jerk. Jeff and I often joked that Lidow, in his arrogance, remained oblivious to how close he really came.

Shop stewards are extremely important people on a construction site, with the most important being the teamster, followed by the operating engineer. I am personally a strong supporter of unions and the union movement, but when it comes to the construction trades, it really is a stretch not to abhor them. The origins of work rules were to prevent bosses from taking advantage of workers. Those days are long gone and union labor on construction projects are some of the highest paying and plummiest jobs you can get. Sure workers work hard, although they get time and a half for every hour over 7 per day that they work, and built into that time is changing time and break time, so they really only work about 5 ½ hours. Also certain trades have a limit on the amount of work they must do in a day, such as tile layers, so theoretically they can finish up in half a day if they work fast. There are also jobs that require a certain number of men to do the task, per the union dictates, such as large pieces of glass. At the Hyatt, we had massive store fronts with 24 man lites. That meant that to handle a pane of glass of a certain size required 24 men, although it was impossible to get more than 8 men on the lite. So the rest stood by and watched. Same for large pipes. A 12" chilled water line required 8 men although only 4 were needed to handle the chain falls. There was a time that building codes were dictated by the unions, so materials that you could safely use outside of NYC were written out of the Code. Over the years, concessions have been made back and forth but by and large, the construction trades are the highest paid of workers and the most powerful. Just another reason why they are male dominated and likely to remain so.

    Unlike the everyday journeyman, the shop steward doesn't do labor, his job is to make sure that the rules are followed. So a teamster steward is out there checking the trucks that deliver materials to the job to insure they have teamster drivers. That is when he is not sitting in his air conditioned on-site shanty with a couch and a bed and a colored TV, well stocked bar, and occasional female visitor.

The operating engineer controls who uses the elevators and the hoists. If you can't get on the hoist, you cannot get material to your workers. In other words, the engineer controls the subcontractor's fate and fortunes. This can be a very lucrative position. This is a very respected and feared man.

The rest of the stewards get their chits too. It is a political appointment, actually no different from the kinds of things you read about with McGreevy and Koch, Spitzer etc. but when it is in your face, you start to resent it. I got along great with all the stewards until a little problem happened with the electricians.

Our first Christmas, we put trees on the balconies of the building, about a dozen or so and we wanted to light them up. We had already given all the lighting on the interior trees and wreaths and railings etc. to the union so that instead of costing $10/hour for the decorators minions to do this, we paid inept electricians who probably don't even do the lights at home $60/hr. for the same work. But they were ignoring me on the outside lights and I wanted them done. I waited a long time, and finally I told my building maintenance workers to string the lights. I figured I would be slapped with a fine like the old days at the Hyatt, and I would have the goddamned trees lit up on 5th Ave before Christmas was over.

Here is what the little prick son of a bitch electrician shop steward did. He got his crones to switch the neutrals in the panels feeding the lights which blew out not only the lights, but the receptacles and the breakers, and could have caused a goddamned fire. I wanted to get the police in to press charges. Donald didn't want to do it. The contractor fixed all the panels, replaced the receptacles and restrung the lights, all out of his own pocket. Big goddamned deal, he was making a fortune on the job anyway. This is something I will never forget. I have never built a non-union job, and probably never will. But I will never feel the same way about the trades.

Days later, the electrician boss showed up with two cases of Dom Perignon as a Christmas present for me. I put a bottle in my bag and gave the other 23 to HRH. We gave them to the laborers at the Christmas party that year. I got that steward off my job – that was my present. I would like to have seen him in jail.

One of the reasons the building was so tall was the fact that it connected the blocks, so you could walk from 5th Ave. to Madison, or to 59th or 58th street all by going through our building. This allowed Donald to build many floors over what normal zoning would permit. He also did two outside parks, one open to 58th and the other open to 59th which gave him extra square footage. Until 9/11 these zoning bonuses had to be accessible to the public from morning to night seven days a week. So it became a sort of inner city promenade.

From the Fifth Avenue doors, guarded by the doormen in Bearskins, you walked past the magnificent and soon to be fake ficus trees, and came to the elevator lobby. There, in front of the elevators that took you up in the retail or to the office section sat a giant salmon colored grand piano which was played by a pianist from the Eddie Duchin Orchestra. The piano was a major draw. Across from the piano, opposite to the elevators was a solid marble bench about 30 feet long, where people could sit. This was all part of the plan that was approved for the through block arcade. It was monumentally successful. Unfortunately, word must have gotten out among the homeless because they came in droves, driving everyone else away. It is kind of comical when you think about it. All this glass and marble in the ultimate tower of opulence, a brilliant musician playing show tunes on this $50,000 piano, and the city's poorest citizens sitting with their paper bags just passing the day. Of course, Donald got security to chase the homeless away, but they kept coming back. So here is what he did. He had the landscapers cover the bench with potted plants. That got us in trouble with the zoning people at the city. So, he ditched the piano player, which was costing a small fortune anyway, and ultimately the piano itself. Without the music the homeless stayed at bay, and those who dared to come in got chased, and the flowers would show up as quickly as they disappeared so it all worked out.

Matt made it all work out. Matt was my head of security. I was in my office at Trump Tower one day when I was summoned across the street to see Donald. It was the fall of 1981, and the US Open was on. Donald told me a story. He said he was in his seat watching the tennis match, and some kids were nearby making trouble. They were sitting in open seats or something and a patron showed up and there was a ruckus and the stadium security wasn't handling it. Donald said he saw this big guy come running from across the stands, grabbed the two trouble makers single handedly and pulled them out of the arena. Now, this is how I heard it, I wasn't there. Donald got the big guy's name. He was a college grad without a full time job working security at the Open. Donald told me to hire him. Because Fred was still watching over my expenses and I already had 4 people working for me, Donald said put him on HRH's payroll, which I did, but Matt worked for me. Personally, I thought he was great. Donald already had a bodyguard, who was an ex-cop and carried a fire arm. Everybody liked him but people resented Matt because he had no credentials other than the legend of the US Open. But I liked him, and that is all that mattered. He was hardworking and he watched people like a hawk. And he was fiercely loyal so I didn't have to worry about him being taken care of by anyone. After the project was finished Matt continued on as head of security and working closely with Donald. At that point, Matt and I were just friends. But while he was under my purview, I never had to worry about trouble. One day, some street protestor, the kind of person who hands out circulars, showed up in front of the building with a big cart full of pamphlets. I think he must have had a license because we complained to the city to no avail. Donald wanted him gone, he was an eyesore. The next day, all his stuff had been moved to another place. Physically. The guy didn't like that so he came back. He got moved again. After the third try, he got the picture. This happened with other annoyances. Matt made them all go away.

Matt eventually became the body guard, got the gun license, and became more buff than he already was. We used to go to the Vertical Club together to work out. He worked on the serious equipment and was quite a specimen. Soon he was head body guard, and then head of all security for all the NY properties, then all the properties. Now I think he is in charge of all construction. I can't imagine how he would know anything much about construction but what the hell, he knew nothing about security when I hired him and turned out to be great at it. I know he knows one thing and that is where all the bodies are buried. Priceless information.

The retail was filling in and making money and the offices were open, but the crown jewel of the building was the Apartment section, and we were falling over ourselves to get that done. Here is who bought apartments at Trump Tower: extremely rich people. This was the Reagan era when dollars were cheap and interest was high. Half of the apartments were going to Europeans.

Also there was a lot of corporate buying. Courtesy of Louise's relationships, Time Warner Co. was taking at least two floors. We had the president of Electra Asylum Records in an L apartment which was the most expensive line except for the multi floor apartments. The head of Atari, the game maker, combined two apartments on a high floor as did other execs.

Then there was Speilberg. Speilberg had a J and a K, together covering 5th avenue from the Park to downtown. MCA owned the Apartment but, whatever the arrangement, it was Steven's. I remember the first time I met him. We all went up in the outside elevator. I had just been to California for the Lina Lee Group and visited Universal Studios. At the entry to Universal was a street wide banner stating, "20 million people have seen ET." I think Speilberg was on the 56th floor or so, and we didn't even have walls up there yet, but he wanted to see his view. Donald never, and I mean never, took anyone to that building without me. When we got to the top, I pointed to the intersection of 5th Avenue and 57th Street and said to Speilberg, "we are going to hang a sign across the street saying, "20 million people have seen Trump Tower."

From that minute on we were friends and I was there every time Steven came to NY and dropped by to check on his progress. His decor was simple and modern. As he described it, it was San Fernando Valley in the sky. He had an Ice Cream Bar in the living room, and the furnishings were in the earth tones, with light woods. Very understated. Except for one thing. He had this space age lighting system complete with state of the art dimming bank and the dining room light fixture was, well I called it, the Star Wars chandelier. It shot light around in colors and was shaped like a space ship.

Simple as the place looked, the construction was complicated. For instance, a paneled wall just looked like it was made of wood. However, flitches had to be hand selected of some exceptionally rare wood that may have looked like oak but it cost 50X as much, and then laminated to underlayments so they could be applied as panels. Another big problem had to do with the joining of the two apartments. There was this guy from MCA who was a true nobody and a big pain in the ass but he got Donald's ear. He was an architect and, according to him only, in charge of all of MCA's work in the building. Because of this asshole insisting we move a wall, and Donald going along, I had to relocate the plumbing and kitchen exhaust for that entire line of apartments above Spielberg's. It was stupid and unnecessary, even though they obviously paid for it. Donald finally told me it was OK to say no to the change, but by then I already had it taken care of.

Whenever Steven came he brought company. More than once, he showed up with George Lucas. Lucas was so incredibly interested in my story of being a woman engineer and being in charge of the building, we didn't even get to speak about what he does. Maybe that was intentional but he was very charming. Steven brought Amy Irving up and boy did I bend her ear. I loved her work and was dying to know if she actually played the piano in The Competition or the guitar in Honeysuckle Rose, but she told me she was just pretending. What a terrific actress and beautiful.

When Indiana Jones was in the theatres, I asked Speilberg if he thought it was similar to Romancing the Stone. But I couldn't remember the name and said Worship the Stone. He told me that was a better name and the picture stunk. He was really funny and non-pretentious. When we finally got the lighting done, he came up to see it and he was really captivated by his dining room fixture. We stood next to each other and the superintendent turned the light on and it took off doing what it did, and Steven said, "Awesome". I looked at him and said, "Totally." I couldn't resist.

Everyone wanted to change their apartments and that took a lot of detailed construction work, and interfered with my progress. I could not allow scores of different contractors working in the building at the same time I was trying to get a Certificate of Occupancy. Donald and I agreed that HRH, which was one of the best builders in the world if you wanted to erect a 68 story building, was not necessarily the choice to do interiors in multimillion dollar apartments. So while I would insist that the major mechanical and structural work by done by me, through HRH, we needed to find a specialty contractor that we could control, who we could tell the buyers that wanted changes before the C of O they must use for the work. HRH recommended some contractors, and I had experience working with the contractors that the retail stores used, so we narrowed it down to a few, and ended up taking the guy that HRH steered us to. The name of the company was Herbert Construction and their experience with this type of thing was legion. The boss, Ted Kohl, took me to see some examples of his work. I went to Park Avenue Penthouses, Olympic Tower and UN Tower, where I saw my first middle eastern toilet, which is basically a trough in the floor. The same apartment had a platinum wall. It was plaster with applied platinum leaf. That wall alone could buy an entire apartment 2 miles north of that building.

  We issued a mandate that went like this. Anyone wishing to make changes to an apartment before the Certificate of Occupancy was issued had to go through me, and had to use my designated contractors. I oversaw every change and approved it. We also recommended architects and decorators, but that did not really matter because the buyers people couldn't do too much harm, as long as my engineers did the mechanicals, and my contractors executed the work. Any change at all had to be cleared by me. I remember a couple that didn't want their wood floor installed. I told them they would have to pay to eliminate it. I was a scoundrel. I explained that we would have to interrupt the sequence and we already had the material stacked in the apartment, so it would have to be removed, etc. etc. I got money from them. I then, of course, made the floor guy give me a credit for not doing the floor.

Donald got a percentage markup on all the work that the new owners did, which I supervised, to remodel their apartments. This amounted to quite a bit of income, which he shared 50/50 with Equitable. Amazingly, he actually gave me a very small percentage of that. I was in a position to make a small fortune if I wanted to be dishonest, but I had always been an honest person and no amount of money was not going to change that. As Donald said, I was "too honest." But I think his sharing this profit in a small (very small) way was an acknowledgment that he appreciated my honesty and my loyalty to the integrity of the building, which was foremost as we executed these changes to the work.

Without a doubt, the most dramatic of the changes to the apartments was for Verina Hixon, reputed to be an heiress, but maybe she was a bit more of a huckster. Verina was the friend that Ivana and I met up with in Monte Carlo. She was supposedly once married to a Texas billionaire. I didn't know much about that relationship, but I knew well about her relationship to John Cody, president of the Teamsters Union in NY.

Verina bought two of the L line apartments, one over the other, and another adjacent apartment on the upper floor. He plan was to put in a swimming pool. She was on the floor below Donald, 65. The pool was made of steel. I had the structural engineer design a concrete frame to accommodate the water weight within the building structural elements. The pool was about 16'x24' and it had jets all around the sides. It had a heater which could raise the temperature though not to the level of a hot tub.

We built the pool for her, and made a lot of other special accommodations, and she paid for them, but she was trouble. I had a few arguments with her and Donald would predictably take her side. Then one time he accused me of taking money from her, which by the way she offered in such a way that I could pretend it had not happened and then went along with the original program. I am sure there were a few people on the job that were on her payroll one way or the other.

At a point in time, Donald had a falling out with her and that is when the fun began. Her friend Cody was very powerful. I had lunch with him once at "21 Club". He had a bodyguard and a coterie. I thought we were just having lunch to discuss Verina's apartment. Instead there were about 8 people there, and we hardly talked. I had met Cody at her apartment once, and I also met him for a drink by myself. I remember asking him about Jimmy Hoffa whom he said he loved dearly. I had no idea that Cody basically controlled everything that when on in NYC construction or that he was such a gangster. Sure, I knew the score when it came to the unions, but I was playing with fire here. I used to joke about it and I remember Irv Fisher admonishing me. He said there was probably a file on me at the FBI just for having lunch with him. HRH covered my ass all the time.

One time, Verina asked Donald to do something for her, and he finally said no. Verina was already very far into Donald for the changes to her apartments, with no end in sight. Verina called up her friend John and the next thing, all deliveries, including concrete, were stopped on all HRH's projects. HRH was frantic. This went on for several days and HRH asked Donald to capitulate. HRH ended up making its own agreement with Cody which included doing work at Verina's apartment. I am sure Donald and Equitable ended up paying for it anyway.

Verina was a character. I remember going into her apartment one day and she had this artwork all over the place. It was really strange. It was all pictures like cartoons of women with bubbles of their thoughts, it reminded me of the love comics of the 1950's that my sister used to get. Turns out they were all original Lichtensteins. Who knew? My guess was Verina was brokering them. She was definitely not the real thing. I lost track of Verina but I know that she ended up bankrupt and thrown out of Trump Tower. As for Cody, he ended up in jail, convicted on 7 counts of racketeering. He was later convicted of attempted murder.

We had several famous people buy apartments and many others look at them. As I said earlier, whenever someone came to see an apartment with either Donald or Louise, I came along. One day Carol Burnett came to see a place.

I didn't recognize her because her hair was gray, but once you took a good look, you could see she was the venerable comedian. She was pretty and very nice. My favorite visitor was President Nixon and his daughter Tricia. They were looking for a place for her. The building was closed in but the apartment floors were still under construction and the hallways in front of the elevator were slightly depressed to allow for finishes. Three times in a row, when the President got into the elevator, he tripped on the edge of the elevator sill. Finally, the next time we got into the elevator, he took me by the arm and said "Be careful, it's easy to trip on this." May not make up for Watergate, but it was kind of endearing.

Johnny Carson bought an apartment. This is very vivid in my mind for two reasons. We had promised a move in date to him and it wasn't looking so good. We got the final inspection the day he was closing and I went personally down to the building department to get a Certificate of Occupancy. I was there before they opened and I explained to the clerk who the apartment was for, and why I needed that CO so urgently. She told me to sit down. About a half hour later, I got up to ask her how things were going. She told me she just had to type it and I should sit down and not bother her anymore. Half hour later I got up again. This time she told me if I got up again, I would not get the CO today. A while later she yelled at me for looking at her. I waited there about 4 hours for that piece of paper and carried it back and met Donald and Johnny in the apartment.

He was carrying a rain coat. Apparently at some time he must have put that coat down because next thing I knew he had left and called back to tell Donald someone stole his raincoat. He was extremely angry. I got a hold of Matt and we tried to ferret out what happened. If it had been taken, Matt would have found out. We decided that Carson probably grabbed a cab when he left Trump Tower and left his goddamned raincoat there. We ended up paying him for it. He was a bit of a shit.

Paula Anka also took an apartment. When I met him, I told him I really liked his hit song, a first in many years, called *Hold Me Til the Morning Comes*. "Paid for this apartment", he said. Another lovely person, and good looking too.

The reader may wonder how celebrities would feel at home, or even safe, in such a notorious and always crowded building, but the answer to that is simple, the entrance to the Apartment building was on 56th Street, and believe me, it was like Fort Knox. To design the Apartment entry, Ivana hired Angelo Donghia, a very hot interior decorator who is now deceased, but whose line of fabrics and furniture is still very popular. He quoted the phrase "Less is more," and meant it and he was able to sell it to Glitz and Blitz Donald, which in itself, was quite a feat. We used two different marbles, both Italian, Antique Verde, a very dark green and Rosso Levante, a dark burgundy with a white vein. We did the ceiling with real gold leaf and the lighting was indirect and low, so the lobby was on the darker side. The seating was burgundy and green velvet couches and there was a centerpiece table that always boasted a magnificent floral display. The lobby was the ultimate in understated elegance.

Donghia also did Donald's place – that is, the first time. After I left The Trump Organization, Donald and Ivana redid the entire apartment, replete with gold leaf and gold chairs and ubiquitous cherubim. But for the first go round, it was a lot more subtle. Donald and Ivana each had a bathroom. His was dark brown marble. Ivana's had a pink onyx that was translucent so it had to be backed with a solid material. Ivana had a humidified and temperature controlled storage closet for her furs. The main stairway was a curved marble and bronze wonder just off the entry from which you could see the living room which was two stories high and the dining room which had an enormous round table. The kitchen counters were absolute black granite, but they used the building standard cabinets. They upgraded the appliances too. They had an elevator to run the three floors. We customized the interior with bronze and fabric.

The Trumps had a real wood burning fireplace, as did Verina below, and a very large skylight which opened into the family room. That room was painted in green and white and filled with plants like a garden. There was a scary stairway to the roof, upon which we had created a landscaped terrace garden. It was a gorgeous triplex, but compared to the apartments Ted Kohl had taken me to see it was very subtle and elegant but not gaudy. (Except the living room was a bit over the top with fake Ivory panels). All in all, it was extremely tasteful and very Donghia. The next incarnation would be designed by the designer who did the casinos and it turned out to be a bad combination of a "high roller suite" and "The Breakers" in Newport.

The fireplace had a flue that went through the roof for exhaust purposes. It is very difficult to put a fireplace in a building because the smoke must be vented with proper materials which generally involve heavy flues. When we were working on the apartment, a strange accident occurred on 57th Street, just East of Fifth Avenue on the west bound side. A truck that had been stopped along the curb was struck by a magnesium beam. When I heard this news, Donald was already in his office conferring with Tony Raffanello and Aldo Rizzo. It seems a beam fell off a building and went right through the truck, fortunately no one was hurt. I think the police had already come by to ask HRH if it was from our building and they said no.

This thing was a 12 foot, maybe 6 or 8 inch magnesium I beam. We had nothing like that on our building. I verified this with Tony and Aldo. There were three buildings under construction at the time in the same general area: AT&T on 56th and Madison and IBM on Madison between 56th and 57th, and ours. Both of those were slightly taller, they were steel structures, and they had stone and glass curtainwalls. The fact that this piece of metal went through the truck meant it came from very high up. "So where did it come from," I asked, and everybody shrugged. Then Aldo piped up and said they were using beams like that on AT&T, maybe it came from there.

If you understood the geography of this part of the city you would know this meant the beam would have had to have flown the equivalent of two city blocks. It didn't seem possible. But they had the beams, I went there and checked it myself, they were using them for some work in the executive offices at the top of the building. The press started calling and I had my story. I called the structural engineer to verify if he thought this was possible and he came up with a companion theory, so I was fairly certain this is what happened and I went out and sold it on the street. Let us say this was received with a degree of incredulity. For instance, there was a cartoon in the local newspaper depicting an I beam with angel's wings beating its way from the ATT tower to 57th and Fifth. My theory was not being taken seriously.

I did not know where it came from. As a precursor to my job as a lawyer, I was creating a plausible theory to divert suspicion from my client. An alternate theory of the crime as it were. Much later, I learned that when they were rigging that massive flue from Verina's fireplace to the roof, they had set up a chain fall on the roof using magnesium beams. It was only up there for a day and I had not seen it. My guess is one of the beams got blown off the roof, they were extremely light and a good wind could take one and carry it. I imagine Donald and his cohorts knew this when I stepped into the office that day. They also knew they could not let me know what really happened because I would tell have to tell it the way it happened. I did most of the press, except for the really big stuff, so it was logical that I would come up with a plan. Donald always said I was "too honest". Worked for him that time. No doubt HRH insurance paid the damages. But we didn't need to have it publicized that stuff was falling off our building.

There was another accident which was really tragic, and which we made no effort to cover up. A piece of glass from the curtain wall was dropped on the terrace long ago and had been cleaned up. But some shards remained and one was lodged in a section of scaffold that was erected on the terrace. When it came time to remove the scaffolds, the glass broke free and fell to the street. Although we had protection over the pedestrian walkway, somehow it got through and struck a man in the head. He was an executive for Ringling Brothers. They got him to the hospital right away, but unfortunately the man died. On this day, one particular reporter brought a camera crew to Trump Tower. They wanted an interview, so they got me. Three times this nasty woman stood in front of me with the mike in my face trying to get me to say that we dropped a window through the sidewalk bridge. I told her what happened exactly the same way, three times, and she finally walked away. The piece with me did not run on the news.

We had two other tragic deaths on the project. The first came when we were removing the sidewalk. There is vault space under the sidewalk and we intended to recapture that for use in the basement, known forever as the Garden Concourse. We were also replacing the entire sidewalk. We hired a company with, irony of ironies, the name Expert Concrete Breakers to do the job. The idea was to cut the steel cantilevered beams and the concrete where it intersected with the building wall, and the sidewalk would fall to the basement floor. Unfortunately, one of the men cutting the concrete fell with the dropping sidewalk. It was equivalent to cutting off a tree branch while standing on the branch. Apparently he must not have known that the steel was already disconnected on the other side.

The last death we had was a suicide. A man went up to the 4th floor of the atrium, stood on the bridge that spans the front of the waterfall and just jumped. He died on the spot. News got out and the press tried to come into the Atrium with their cameras. Even though technically I was not in charge of the building at this time, I got a hold of Matt and told him, no press and there was no press. At the time there was a commercial running on television showing a man diving into a swimming pool as the narrator said, "Take a refreshing Nestea Plunge". This tragedy became known as the TT Plunge, just as the prior tragedy was satirized as the work of Concrete Experts. This was gallows humor.

Every day you walk on to a construction site, you are assuming a level of risk and humor is one way of dealing with it. Construction workers have a higher yearly death rate than police officers. Accidents happen no matter how hard you try to prevent them. Fortunately, rules and protections are more stringent now than ever, but you have to follow them. HRH never broke a protection rule, nor did any company I ever worked with on one of my jobs. For most builders, safety is sacrosanct. Still, one morning in June 1981, we were removing the street crane from the project, and the operator dropped the boom. It fell right down on the stretch of road we had closed off along 56th street. No one was hurt. About 4 hours later, the streets were filled with pedestrians arriving early for the Puerto Rican Day Parade. Had it fallen later, it would have been a disaster. Looking back to my own accident, it's a good thing I didn't get killed when I fell off the ledge at the Hyatt ballroom – it would have set women in construction back 100 years. Gallows humor.

During the process of finishing and opening the apartment building, we had a few small fires and a lot of false alarms. I remember seeing the firefighters arrive one day with axes out ready to break down our bronze door to the Fire Command Center because it was locked from the inside. While I had someone rush around the building to get it opened, I convinced them to hold the axes at bay. Another time, I was up in Donald's apartment checking on something when I got a call on my walkie talkie that there was a fire alarm in the building and the Fire Department had shut the elevators down. There I was, all alone on the 68th Floor, and I had to fend for myself. The emergency generator was working and there was light in the stairwells. I walked/ran down the stairs, in my bare feet because, by then, I was dressing like an executive and had high heels.

I was not uncomfortable being stranded up there, forced to figure out things for myself. I often went up to the top, after everyone was gone, and just looked down at the city. Even when it was bare concrete, and the only barrier was a steel wire. I liked the feeling of being on top of the world, and, to my mind, I *was* on top of the construction world. I made that climb alone. And in those moments, I reveled in what I had accomplished. I always managed to find my way back, and the day of the fire alarm, somehow, I got to the lobby, soon enough, to deal with the Fire Department. I dealt with my feet for several days after that.

Now the building was fully open and Donald decided we needed a Building Manager. Donald hired someone from Tiffany, the building next door, who was very classy, according to Donald, and highly recommended. The man was OK but frankly, he didn't really get it. He didn't know anything about construction and Jeff and I thought he was very bad with people. Nobody liked him.

During the construction period, we negotiated with a few building management companies to provide porters. We also had a specialty metal polishing contractors and marble finishing companies. I made the selections based on price and Jeff's interviews, Donald had final approval, and I had Jeff supervise the operations. To be honest, I never thought we needed anyone else. We were already running the building and doing a good job at it. We hired a building superintendent while we were under construction in the apartments. He had his own apartment at Trump Tower and knew the ropes. He was one of the team. We all fell in together and were tight knit. I had John Re on mechanical, Matt on security, Jeff was supervising the Atrium and tenants, John Dalessio was on the apartment construction, John Hughes was the superintendent, Roberta intersected with all the leads and Jeanne was there to help her. Everyone worked under me. Then all of a sudden we got the new guy.

From the start, we told Donald about him. Donald coined a new phrase for me, in his mind, the ultimate criticism. "You know what's wrong with you?", he said, "you want people to like you." He was right. Of course, if people hated me that building would have still been half empty because we were like soldiers and I was the general and we constantly had to advance like crazy. You cannot get the kind of dedication and sacrifice out of soldiers who do not love and respect their generals.

This is a problem with many very rich people and big bosses. They don't fully get the concept that to get someone to work 48 hours round the clock, they *have* to like you. Donald got more out of us because of the relationship we had then he would have with twice as many people. But he probably knew that. He was just giving me shit. "People like you to much." Ha, then he goes around telling the world how his people love him. At that time, I certainly was devoted to him and he mostly paid me back with respect and even affection. (This humanity unfortunately faded as Donald's star brightened.) No matter, at my insistence, he dismissed the guy who was just wrong for us. I suggested Jeff run the building and Roberta be his right hand, and that is exactly what we did, and it worked for a very long time. Ultimately, John Re took over the management responsibilities as Jeff moved on. Basically, the way I planned it.

That was not the first time Donald made a hiring mistake. When we were in the swing of construction, Donald came across a candidate for apartment building superintendent. I think he may have come from Fred or the people in Brooklyn. Anyway, he was German, and as with most nationalities, Donald had a sense of the value of Germans and he believed it was in building management because they were very clean and thorough to a fault. Only this guy was very useless. He knew zero about construction and offered no assistance to me or Jeff. Plus he had very annoying habits, and since Jeff had to share his office with the guy, it drove him nuts. It took about 2 weeks for us to figure out this guy had to go. To be honest, it was absurd for Donald to just hire someone without having me interview him first, or Louise, since this guy was supposed to be the person who interacted with the super rich apartment owners. He had zero personality. He might have been perfect for a building in Brooklyn, but not Trump Tower. Jeff and I went to see Donald to tell him he had to go. "OK." Donald said, "Fire him." Being better at this kind of thing than I was, I asked Jeff to do it, and he did, nicely, but firmly. Next thing we know, the guy marches across the street to Donald's office and gets himself rehired. I went nuts. Donald said we didn't really give the guy a chance. It took two more firings for it to stick. Maybe Donald can unceremoniously say, "You're fired" to actors on a TV show, but in real life, he hated to do it. When someone had to be fired, Donald laid the job off on an underling. We always felt that if you were close enough to Donald that he would have to be the one to let you go, you had a job for life.

It was during Jeff's tenure as building manager that we had most of the Atrium parties. One of the extravaganzas was for Donald to audition cheerleaders for his newly purchased football team, the New Jersey Generals. They had scores of beautiful young women come in and work with a choreographer and did their tryout routines in the atrium at the base of the waterfall. They danced to Michael Jackson music which we had blasting in the atrium. We also had these massive lights which were connected to the outlets in the planters, which were never intended for that purpose. Sure enough, we blew out the power. Now, I didn't even have to attend this event because technically I was not in charge of the building. Fortunately I was there. Given the level of detail I used to torture the electrician into lowering his price, I had intimate knowledge of the power in the atrium and knew just how to fix it. And we did. John and Jeff had lots of crazy parties there after I left, with live animals and all sorts of celebrities. Trump Tower Atrium was hot for a long time as an event venue.

With most of the construction work done, and no new building on the horizon for Donald, I started getting a little itchy. Now I had office tenants with tiny spaces wasting my time on bullshit problems and acting like jerks with me, when I would have blown them off a year earlier. I could have stayed with Donald for the rest of my life, but I was restless and I wanted to do another big job. I found a position with promise of a financial interest in a project in Staten Island, so I decided to leave. Donald wanted me to stay but we both knew that it would be some time before he had anything major, and I would get bored. He threw me a great party in the office and gave me a going away present - a beautiful bracelet from Cartier engraved with the words, "Towers of Thanks, Love, Donald"

Chapter 10 - The Other Real World

I went off to Staten Island, which is something no one should ever do. With the exception of learning about floating docks and dredging, which was fun, it was a totally useless experience and I would rather forget those 4 months. The job was canceled, I got two weeks' pay, and I had to find a job again.

Naturally, I went to Artie. He wanted to use me as Project Manager on a big building down at the World Trade Center; I think it was the American Express Building. So he put my name up for consideration. My old friend Ted Kohl from Herbert Construction had wangled the position of Construction Manager for his company at the building, through his relationship with one of the top executives of American Express, so HRH was really only a general contractor there. Much later, we learned of some real shenanigans Kohl had pulled at this building, but at the time, I just thought he wanted to keep utmost control over the site, and to maintain a bit of secrecy, because when Artie put my name up, he said flat out – NO.

I was shocked, Ted was my friend. But I could understand. He knew me extremely well. If I was on the job, whatever he intended to pull would not go unnoticed, or unreported. I had seen Ted "take care" of contractors, workers, owners, bosses, etc. during my relationship with him at Trump Tower. I protected my building and probably cost him a good deal of money at the time. As a matter of fact, the project that ultimately led to his arrest was the new Asprey store at Trump Tower, built long after I left. One thing Ted was not going to do was let me come in to this project as head of HRH's team and muck up the works. So he came up with some cockamamie excuse, like saying the owner wanted someone with a different background - I don't remember but we all knew it was bullshit at the time, and I lost that job. That was all Artie had at the time. Plus he was still pissed off at me for going to Trump so he wasn't going out of his way to help me. Artie never got over me leaving him.

I was really close with Ted and he knew I was livid. So he did me a favor. His personal friend, Leonard Stern, was the owner of Hartz Mountain Industries which was not only the pet food business, but a New Jersey Real Estate development empire owning millions of feet in retail, housing and commercial ventures. Leonard was making his first foray into New York City with an office building on 61 Street and Madison, right on the edge of a special historic zoning district, which made his the last tall building on that part of the East Side. Leonard already had HRH building the project, which, at the time was in demolition, and he did not have an owner's project manager. Ted called him and said there was only one person to do the job, and that was Barbara Res. Hartz interviewed me twice and I had the job as Vice President for construction of the New York Headquarters. I had another job offer by then but it was to build an ordinary apartment building for a colorless owner. I liked the idea of working for Hartz and the building he designed had a lot of cache. I made the right decision going to Leonard.

We had an existing building to take down and replace with a beautiful modern building which was designed to evoke the architectural sensibilities of the area. There were also a few brownstones on the property and one of them was being used by HRH for its field offices. Hartz Mountain had office space in a building on Madison one block away.

HRH had just begun buying out the trades which, after having finished Trump Tower, was my specialty. (Remember, I learned at the foot of an old master – Fred Trump, god help me.) So I jumped right into the project and liked it. Leonard was not involved on a daily basis, the way Donald had been, but he was around frequently and made decisions. I think he was, of all my bosses, the one who treated me the best. He never second guessed my decisions, and he didn't grill me. Although it was technically Leonard's money I was spending, he was a little distanced from the day to day in most of his business and he trusted the people who worked for him, including myself. This was the closest thing to owning my own building.

I started that job in April. Around the beginning of June, we had the building down and were digging the hole. We made some progress and then we stopped. This was one of the most frustrating experiences of my life. We had bought out most of the major trades, the steel was being made, but we were stuck in the hole. Civetta was the contractor doing the excavations and foundations, and Guido Civetta was the owner's name. I was watching as the activity dwindled down to a halt. HRH blamed everything on Guido and I would call a meeting and yell at Guido and then everyone would go away and nothing happened. In retrospect, I suspect Leonard knew what was going on. I didn't initially know but soon found out that there was a time limit for a special program for subsidized housing being built in NY and foundations had to be completed before a certain date or the building could not qualify for lucrative tax incentives. (Here is a note of irony. This program was to spur development so the tax deferrals actually went to millionaires who bought apartments in the luxury buildings that were covered under this plan. Trump Tower had a 20 year reduced tax incentive that made the real estate taxes on the expensive apartments almost nothing.) HRH had lots of these buildings in foundation, many with Civetta, so they just decided they were going to put their resources where they would do the most good. We ended up with no equipment at all on our site for a few weeks, and me screaming for the entire time. This is one of the disadvantages of going with a big construction company. You become just one of their many jobs, and their divided loyalties can cost you. With Trump HRH had a history and more importantly, there was a big future. Donald would be building many more jobs and HRH wanted to do them, so his work got special attention Whereas, Hartz Mountain was a one shot deal. It is probably true that much of the service we managed to get out of HRH was due to my personal relationships and my influence on others in the industry as well, as the likelihood that *I* would be deciding on who did the work for other owners in the future. But neither I nor Leonard Stern nor the power of Hartz Mountain could get our foundation going until after that deadline.

      Civetta's delay cost us a good month and a half on our schedule. I was going to try to make that up as much as possible. The building was steel. Most office buildings are made of steel and steel takes a lot of preparation as opposed to concrete which you can change ten minutes before you pour it. So while we were delayed in the foundation, the steel drawings were progressing and the steel was being made so we were able to get a jump on the erection and picked up some time there. Also, the other trades were all progressing in their shop drawings so we were able to do the coordination and other things well in advance, and avoid the mistakes and costs you encounter when you're rushing through on a fast track.

      The Hartz Mountain building was on the edge of the historical district in New York City. Anything north of us had special Zoning restrictions, so our building dominates the skyline looking south. It was designed to fit in with the other buildings in the area. The building we replaced was about 10 stories. Ours would reach over 300 feet.

      We had demolished two brownstones with the building and we had a third one where we located HRH's field offices. That brownstone was later sold and became the home of one of New York's finest restaurants. Hartz had its offices in a modern office building a block away. Once the building got closed in, I moved into an office shanty on site.

The building was to be a curtainwall of glass and granite with a limestone base. The granite was supposed to come from Italy. The architect, with our wall consultant, was proposing using a granite of a narrower depth than was the usual application on a building application. This was because the design of the aluminum structure that would hold it in place has a stronger structural nature. We needed to get a special approval which required a little schmoozing with the building department, but we got the go ahead, and many other walls were done this way afterwards. However, even with the lighter stone, the material HRH had proposed was extremely expensive. One of the bidders came up with an alternative which looked like the sample the architect suggested but it was much less money. It was from Spain and called Mondariz, a pink and grey granite. The architect was satisfied with the look of it. We bought the curtainwall from a company called FEI that built its panels in Ireland. As part of the due diligence that is usually performed, we visited the factory in Ireland, and also went to Spain to look at the granite.

I had a problem in planning the trip though. I had only just found out I was going to have a baby, twins actually, and I didn't want to tell anyone until after I had gone a few months and knew the pregnancy was viable. I didn't care if people thought I gained a few pounds. The last thing I wanted was to tell everyone I was pregnant and then lose the baby and I was having trouble from the very beginning. I was well aware of the conjecture that would immediately arise, and I didn't want the world to know my business until it was absolutely necessary. However, I decided if I was going to travel in the first trimester I should tell one of my companions, just to be safe. Unfortunately, I picked the biggest mouth in construction to share my confidence with.

The trip to Europe was hectic. First we flew to Ireland to see the factory. I had been to the aluminum plant for the curtainwall at Trump Tower but this was entirely different. The stone was to be cut into slabs in Spain and then shipped to Ireland for installation into the framework. The panels would be attached to the steel and then glazed in the field. The entire assembly of the panel was a structural element. The factory was extremely well run and efficient. I was very satisfied that we had chosen a contractor who could do a quality job. Ireland was very cold, in July, and rainy. Next, we went to Vigo in Spain, a lovely coastal town near the town of Mondariz where the stone was quarried. As with Carrera, everything was paved in granite. Unlike Carrera, it was all one color, the lovely pink and gray. Paving stones, stone walls, the stones that homes were built from were all the same.

I met the owners of the quarry and they took us to lunch in a castle. I especially remember this lunch because we at an enormous table and after we were finished the waiters walked in with a box of cigars for the gentlemen. Since I always hated cigar smoke, and particularly because I was pregnant, I left the room and wandered out on the terrace which overlooked the mountains from which the stone was taken on one side and the sea on the other. This is one of the most beautiful places I have ever been.

Although much smaller than Trump Tower, the Hartz Mountain project was challenging in many ways, and I had direct control on a day to day basis, that is, once the design was concluded, Leonard Stern was rarely on the job, nor did he attend any job meetings with the contractors. He met with the Architect, on occasion, and also met once or twice with prospective tenants and the bank. Some of the most difficult elements of this project did not have to do with men or materials, they had to do with the subcontractors' financial status.

I had two subs going under on the job. The first situation was the most critical because he was literally shutting his doors. This was a company called Heritage Iron Works and they did what is known as Ornamental Iron. Heritage was responsible for the storefronts, and also many elements of the interior of the Lobby including the very decorative metal door fronts on the elevators and all the glass and mirror. The owner of this company was a character in his own way, he carried a revolver in a strap around his ankle, just inside his cowboy boot. He also wore a cowboy hat. Although his shop was in Connecticut, I think he originally came from Texas.

  At a point in time, HRH announced to us that he was going broke. They told me that his bonds had already been called in on two other projects. I didn't have a bond, nor did I want one. Also, I didn't care who installed the work, ironworkers are ironworkers and glazers are glazers, I could always get the labor. What I cared about was our intricate metalwork that was in fabrication at the time. I told HRH to find a warehouse up there near his shop. We got the space. I arranged for Heritage to walk each piece it made out the door and into our warehouse as it was finished. I paid them for the materials, one by one, to keep him alive, and bought special insurance to cover us for the time the pieces were in storage and in freight. Because we were paying directly, we got immediate attention. The owner, whose name escapes me, was beside himself. He was losing his company. HRH was worried that he might pull that gun on himself. I spoke with him as often as I could and we had a man sitting up there in Connecticut watching our pieces. Finally, after our last piece was made, it was the day before Thanksgiving in 1986, Heritage closed its doors. We got the sub that was installing the exterior panels as part of the curtainwall contract to pick up the ornamental iron installation, and the glazer to do the glass. It cost us a premium over what we had originally planned to pay Heritage, but we did not lose a minute. Had we needed another manufacturer to tool up to make our pieces, it would have cost us months.

The next big problem I had was with the windowwall guy. The guy from Ireland. He did a big job on the Hudson River in NY for an owner that had over extended itself, and was not able to keep him current. FEI was losing money. Actually, they were just not getting paid, and were struggling. We knew he was in trouble but he was on the job working. The curtainwall was difficult and our inspector, the engineer who was to sign off on the job was giving him a particularly hard time. It was all the complaining I was getting from Fogerty, the owner of FEI that led me to sniff out that there was something else wrong besides arguments over one eighth inch gaps in the exterior. I shortly learned that John had not been paying the IRS and he was in major trouble. The government was going to force him into bankruptcy. We immediately got a hold of the IRS, and along with FEI, agreed that we would take over the ironworker's payroll and make the payments to the IRS directly along with the payments to the workers. FEI had their problems on other sites, but since we were covering the labor situation, they were able to finish our work. I also think that the relationship between Fogerty and I had something to do with our ability to get the job completed. All the materials were delivered to the site and we were able to assume the subcontract for the glass installation and take that away from FEI. So, this contractor, too, closed its doors when our project was finished.

We also had some problems with the elevator company. I was used to working with Otis and Westinghouse. Nowadays there are lots of elevator companies but when our job was bought there were only a few, and we gave the contract to a Japanese company, Fujitec, that was breaking into the US market, and had bid the job very competitively. I had no knowledge of the customs of the Japanese and did not know of their national sexism. So when the officials came into the office I gave them a mouthful of choice words for being behind their schedule, like I would with any other sub. I relish at the thought of this now, knowing how it must have killed these guys having to take a tongue-lashing from a woman.

Truth was that they were holding us up and it only got worse. A common practice at the time was "taking care" of the inspectors. I don't think this goes on anymore, I hope not, but at the time, it was expected that the contractor would make an elevator inspection happen and get the certificate of occupancy so you could open the building, whatever it took. Fujitec did not want to play. This fact astounded me because of the legacy of corruption in Japan. When faced with this, I, who had made a cottage industry of avoiding anything untoward, reminded HRH that it was their job to make sure we got a C of O for the elevators and they did. I am sure that Fujitec ultimately paid for the privilege and I have no doubt that they soon became quite adept at the ropes, as this time was the dawn of the Japanese foray into American Real Estate which lasted for many years, during which we had to hear all the crap about paternalism and buying for the next generation and how the Japanese were all so brilliant, which I knew was all bullshit, until it finally blew up in their faces.

This project was very successful. When it was completed, it was financed at substantially more than the cost of the project including the land. So the owners were able to take out the initial investment plus a substantial cash profit of millions of dollars, and retain a profitable office building which grew dramatically in value over the next 25 years.

The owner of the building was Hartz Mountain but the main tenant was Loew's Hotels, so they were named on the glass door at the entrance to the building. However, Leonard Stern had a corner stone installed on the east side of the front entrance and in the granite was inscribed the following: Hartz Mountain Developer - Leonard Stern, John Halpern, Barbara Res; Paul Helpern - Architect 1985. This is still there and will always be, right there next to the fancy restaurant which was recently replaced with a division of Sotheby's International Real Estate.

When the building was ready, Leonard and company, including me, moved into beautiful offices on the top floor. I had an unobstructed view looking north. Yes, I had this beautiful room but the project was basically finished, and as with Trump Tower, I didn't want to be the relief pitcher, dealing with the tenants and their crap. I was a starter. I got the wanderlust. So I called Donald to see what he was up to. He asked me to come over and of course I did.

Donald hired me. Donald and Leonard had a bit of a rivalry going on at the time that escalated into something ugly courtesy of Donald, who attacked Leonard's wife in the press. I had heard a rumor that Donald at one time had tried to force Louise out of her partnership interest in Trump Tower by making her pay $1 million in taxes which she did not have sitting around. Leonard, who was Louise's really close friend, and an extremely wealthy man, put up the money for Louise and she kept her significant piece of Trump Tower. Rich people play treacherous games. Donald and Louise worked out their differences over time, but I can't say there's any good feeling between Donald and Leonard. Leonard was probably not thrilled at me having been stolen from him by his rival, but he threw a big party for my going away and gave me the most incredible string of huge pearls as a parting gift.

I appreciated Leonard, and often say of my bosses, he was the most generous. There is nothing anyone can ever give me that will diminish having my name carved in the stone at the front of the building. That was priceless!

Chapter 11 - Back Where I Belong

It was June, 1987. Working for Donald again, after having built the new Hartz Mountain Building, was a very different experience from the early days. By now, Donald was an institution. He had two casinos under his belt, and another apartment building on Central Park West, a conversion of the old Barbizon Hotel. He was in the Trump Office for a few years already and had surrounded himself with a new coterie of executives, most of them lawyers. He had hired the man at HPD that had given Donald such a hard time about getting the tax exemption for Trump Tower, to work on development of what we called the West Side Railyards, which we then called "Trump City", and later became "Riverside South". There was a new lawyer, Joe something, who, from what we could tell, existed for sole the purpose of protecting the Trump name from being used for anyone else's purpose except Donald, like a copyright and trademarks guy. Another woman, Susan, a Yale lawyer, was involved in Donald's investments including overseeing the filing of SEC forms, which he had to do when he accumulated a percentage of a company's stock. She also watched the market, curiously interrupting Donald every hour on the hour to give him quotes on his stocks, no matter who was in the office and what he was meeting about. She would walk in, hand him a yellow piece of paper and walk out. Susan was one of the smartest people I ever met, and she would be a big factor in Trump's acquisition of the Merv. Griffin Hotel,

Resorts International which became the Taj Mahal. But for the time, she made that little hourly foray and as a result, she always knew exactly what Donald was doing, who he was seeing, and what was being discussed every day. I learned from Susan to check the fax machine often, and since I was there earlier and later than most people, I often got the scoop on what Donald was doing. They eventually moved Donald's fax to his office, but I spied on that too, because, as I said, I was there before anyone else.

Then there were the utility lawyers, in house real estate, casino and development lawyers who rounded out the rest of the staff. Along with a woman who sold apartments, and myself, this was the Trump Dream Team. Donald had 3 or 4 secretaries, a security detail, instead of the one guy I had hired on Trump Tower, an entire accounting department, imported directly from Brooklyn, and an in house decorator and architect who worked exclusively with Ivana on the casinos. There was also a land planner that came with the package when Donald bought the rail yards. All and all, a cozy bunch of backstabbing cutthroats, nothing less than you would expect.

I wasn't there very long before I imported my former secretary Cecelia from Hartz Mountain and brought back my trusty sidekick J. Jeffrey Walker who was managing someone else's property portfolio. This was a new Trump Organization, with more glitz, money, a lot more egos, more fancy parties, and for the most part, a different work effort. Gone were the days when

DJT and I would hold down the fort at 7:00AM. He was never alone anymore and even though he lived in the building, he started his day at home and came in much later. Working in an office on construction and working on a construction site are extremely different things. This was nicer, although not as fun. In June 1987, I came on board as an Executive Vice President at $200,000 with full benefits, a brand new red BMW 535is, lots of perks, a large office, specially built for me, and a bonus.

My first job was to oversee the Alexander's projects. Alexander's was a failing department store with great real estate. The plan was to close some of all of the stores and exploit the real estate. As a public company, Alexander's stock traded on the open market. Donald and a much quieter but very canny NJ Developer named Steve Roth, each owned enough stock that together they had a controlling share. There was an agreement between them that Donald would be the front man in the development efforts, which put me in charge of what happened to Alexander's.

Alexander's already had a project at the city awaiting approval. It was going to be a mall in Rego Park, Queens where a single store was already standing. They had sketched out drawings and plans for a Sears as one anchor with Alexander's on the other side. We needed a special franchise agreement to build a bridge across a street to connect the two sides of the shopping center. The first thing I did was go out and hire a new architect, put together a team with a construction manager and find new stores. Sears was staying but Alexander's was not. We all knew that Alexander's was a real estate play.

Alexander's also owned one of the best pieces of property in the mall capital of the world - Paramus, New Jersey, and Donald wanted to put a mixed use development there that we could call Trump Centre. That was also going to be the name for the one in Queens, Trump Centre. Looking back, I realize that I learned the retail development business by working on Alexander's and Donald got them to pay for it too. Robin Farkas was the Chairman and a major stockholder in the company. His father started the company with the store in the Bronx, which he named for his father, Alexander. Farkas and I hit it off immediately. There was the store in the Bronx, two in shopping centers in Long Island, one in a power mall in Westchester, one in a downtrodden godforsaken mall in New Jersey, they owned the Brooklyn shopping center Kings Plaza, there was a White Plains store, a store in the World Trade Center and, of course, the crown jewel, Lexington Avenue in New York. The NY store is where the Bloomberg Building now stands, but it went through probably 200 design iterations before Roth got Bloomberg involved in the early 2000s.

Just before I started, Donald had somehow brokered a deal to sell one of the properties and collected a commission of several hundred thousand dollars on the sale. There was a second property they wanted to unload but they were nowhere with negotiations because the owner of the mall the store was located in was intransigent. It was the store in Menlo Park New Jersey. The ugliest store I ever saw. J.W. O'Connor was playing real hard ball stating he would just let us pay rent until the lease ran out in 7 years, and then tear it down.

That mall had just been bought by JW O'Connor Company which was going to build a luxury Shopping Center. Because that was the thing then, luxury shopping centers. I was going to be doing at least three of these myself, so I learned all about these high end specialties the hard way. Well, it wasn't so hard. I just went all over the place and looked at them. I got to know all the retailers, all the big players, what the going rents were in various places, who the top architects were, what kind of vendors you put where, etc. I reached a point where I was quoted in *Shopping Center Weekly*, as a retail expert. I wouldn't say that, but I can tell you Jeff and I went all over the country - California, Texas, Massachusetts, Illinois, DC, Washington, Michigan, Florida, Georgia, plus we combed every inch of the tri-state area. I was on a first name basis with the owners of stores like Nordstrom's. As a matter of fact, I personally drove Bruce Nordstrom all over the NY/NJ retail meccas in the hope of trying to attract them to our new malls in Manhattan, Paramus and Rego Park. These guys, and there were 4 or 5 of them, were the hottest thing in retail at the time and everyone wanted them. But they were literally afraid of

New York. We wanted Nordstrom to anchor a vertical shopping center at the Lexington Avenue location. Across the street was the iconic Bloomingdales which is a world famous fashion haven. We were also in talks with Bloomingdales to connect to their store somehow to our mall through the basement. Our building on Lexington and 59th would be a Chicago Water Tower type building with a massive mall, office space over that, hotel and then apartments at the very top. Kevin Roche the architect did at least 60 versions of a design for this.

  I also had a mixed use center in planning in Paramus and I wanted Nordstrom there. I hired RTKL out of Houston, to do the plan. We had a luxury hotel, I was talking to Four Seasons and Ritz Carlton. There would be a shopping center anchored by Nordstrom and Neiman Marcus. I was in talks to move Lord and Taylor out of another location for a third spot, I also wanted them for Rego Park. The mall would be topped with the hotel and an office building in between. It was to be the first of its kind in Paramus. I found a developer's lawyer, by the name of Tom Wells, who helped us design a plan of attack for zoning approvals. However, we had huge opposition.

  Opposition takes two forms in development projects. You have the real opposition which are interested, if not wrong-headed local citizens, who think what you are doing is not good for the community, and then you have the funding opposition which is your competition who finds a way to either stimulate, or actually pay the opposition that has standing to challenge you. There is always a "Concerned Citizens of Wherever", and a big business that pays for its lawyers. The opposition in Paramus was Westfield, owner of Garden State Plaza, which was in the process of getting approvals for an expansion and after the same tenants.

I spent a lot of my time trying to make a deal on that Menlo Park eyesore. I schmoozed up the head of real estate for O'Connor, and I met with Jerry O'Connor a few times as well. The situation was that Alexander's had a lease with about 7 or 8 years left on it. Nothing they could do or say could force us out of that lease. They wanted our spot for Nordstrom and were willing to let O'Connor buy us out of our lease, they just would not pay what I wanted, which was $20 million. I had a bet with Robin Farkas that I could get the $20. He said the most I would get was $10 million and Alexander's was more than happy to take that. I told Donald about the bet and Donald agreed that if I got more than $10 million, he would give me a piece of his commission which was 4% of whatever the sale amount was.

I played hard ball with O'Connor and let them know I was in with Nordstrom which was the company they desperately wanted that location for. They threatened to challenge the lease but I stood firm that the lease was iron-clad, and all we had to do was keep paying the small rent. To my mind, I could have done a better job than O'Connor. I am sure that they could have forced

Alexander's into doing some maintenance work or gone over the books with a fine tooth comb, but these guys wanted us out so bad, that once I convinced them that we were not moving on the price, they capitulated. I sold that lease to J.W. O'Connor Company for $20 million. Farkas bought me lunch. But my big payoff was coming from Donald.

I asked Farkas to give the check to me personally when it was ready for Donald and he did it. I took that check and waltzed into Donald's office and handed it to him and he asked me what it was, and I explained it. He immediately became enraged. "Why did they give it to you?" I explained that I asked Farkas to do that because I was the one who made the deal and I wanted to give it to Donald because he had promised to give me some of the commission. Donald did not even know who I sold the lease to, or whether it was a lease or a fee. He referred to the buyer as the Irishman. But that did not matter, because I was just doing my job and the money was his and he said I was way out of line having Farkas give me the check and so was Farkas. So Donald got his $800,000 and Farkas and Alexander's got their $20,000,000 (10 million more than they expected or were probably entitled to) and what did I get? I got chewed out. A lesson about rich people. They didn't get rich by giving things away. Of all the times Donald screwed me over, this one hurt the most because I really believed he would give me something for this and I had broken my ass to make it happen. The one thing that I got which no one can take away was the experience of negotiating such a difficult deal. Thanks, Donald, Robin.

Besides the Alexander's projects, I also worked on the West Side Yards. This was a sink hole of a project that had been languishing at the New York City Department of Environmental Protection for at least 4 years despite the power team we had trying to cut it loose. Donald hired Tony Gliedman to head up this project and that was a massive assignment, which would require taking it through the City approval process along with special approvals from the FAA and the New York State Departments of Environmental Protection and Transportation along with all the city agencies. Formerly known to us as the "fat fuck" who held up Donald's tax abatement on Trump Tower, Tony, now to be our savior, – was a player in the Koch Administration and had an incredible amount of clout. One of my Alexander's projects was in Queens and Tony connected me with the borough president and the head of the city council. He was also a tennis buddy of the later to be Mayor, David Dinkins. I was able to get clearance to build a connector between two buildings over a city street in Queens and that was all thanks to Tony. This is an incredibly difficult approval to get because it involves several departments. Tony had the juice.

It proved to take more to budge the NYCDEP than just connections though. We were requesting a zoning change which requires a Land Use Review Process which brings in everybody form the community review boards to the City Council. We had to do an exhaustive Environmental Impact Report which took years to complete. Among other onerous tasks, it required analyzing traffic impacts miles away.

For environmental lawyers, Donald got Berle, Cass and Cates. These were the lawyers that stopped the West Side Highway project cold over a fish. Bringing them on was not only to handle the myriad of environmental issues we were plagued with at the rail site, but to co-opt the opposition from hiring them, an extremely smart move. Opposition was rife. We had a lot of big names fighting us, major local and national organizations and celebrities like Steve Reeves.

The biggest obstacle was the DEP. We worked very closely with them and every time we thought we had covered all the possible impacts, they would come up with something new to study. The object of an Environmental Impact Report is to state every possible impact your project may cause to the environment and then you need to come up with a way to mitigate it or demonstrate that even though the impact cannot be mitigated, you project is so important to the city that it will withstand the impact. For instance, if you are bringing millions of dollars of tax income to the city, it might be willing to take a traffic impact. Of course, you work around impacts by agreeing to do things, such as build a new subway station, or pay for traffic improvements. The city is supposed to pass your application through in a certain time period. However, if they want to hold you up, they can keep asking for things and if you don't agree to provide them or force the issue, the city will just deny your application and you are back to square one. At the end of the day, when the city finally approves a project, it does so by certifying the Environmental Impact Report. At that time, the Report is now their own and anyone who wants to sue, actually has to sue the city or what they call the lead agency, which in our case was the DEP of New York.

Our opposition was too powerful and very well organized. There were seven or eight organizations established just to fight us and then there were the local and national big names. We were up against formidable resources and they had control over the DEP, it was obvious.

While Tony was the head of the project, I was in charge of anything having to do with construction. There were several mounds or piles of dirt that had been placed in different locations over the history of that 70+ acre site and they became important around the end of 1988. Supposedly, no one knew where they came from. But that was all bullshit, because, at least the guy we inherited from the original owner must have known because he was there when it happened. And he was too minor in the organization to keep this information to himself. Doubtless, he told Gliedman and probably Donald's brother Robert, as well.

I have always speculated that the original owner made a lot of money by allowing this dumping to occur. We had the soils sampled and tested for contaminants previously by engineer and laboratory. I saw the reports. The soil was clean. At least the samples that were taken were clean. Now, all of a sudden these piles were hot, figuratively if not literally. I was told to get rid of the piles.

Hmmm . . . . what we had estimated at a half a million yards of questionable material had to go away. The price for dumping contaminated soil back in those days was about $50/yard. But you could bring clean soil to the landfill in Staten Island provided it met certain criteria, which could be proven through a testing process. We hired Dames and Moore to test the soil anew. As it happened, the soil turned out to be clean enough to use as fill at the landfill.

The landfill is now closed. At the time it took three types of material. Fill was dump material and you paid to bring it there. Roadway materials were fill that had sufficient rock and brick in it to make it useful for this purpose and you could bring it to the landfill for free. Then there was cover. Cover was what the put on the top of the fill when they were finished loading a section of the landfill. Cover was clean stuff and it was laid on heavy over the fill and debris and finished off the top of the dump. The Department of Sanitation *paid* for cover. So I wanted to use our stuff as cover. No way I was told. The best I could hope for was fill. So I was faced with what looked to be a $2 million cleanup job.

I went to our general contractor HRH Construction who had built Trump Tower and the

Hyatt for Donald, and the Hartz Mountain building for me, so I knew them very well. They had no idea what to do, and upon reflection, I now understand HRH just did not want any part of it. They referred me to a young kid, Frankie, about 27 years old, who owned an excavation company and some trucks and had a contract with Fresh Kills dump in Staten Island. I asked for some other contractors but I couldn't get anyone to give me a decent price. HRH, which had done a billions of dollars' worth of construction work, couldn't find us a contractor. The kid, it turned out, did not, himself, have a contract with the Department of Sanitation, but I really liked him and had gotten a very good reference on him from my brother in law Vic. Frankie said he had the trucks and would make arrangements for the landfill but reiterated that I could not sell the soil as cover, it would have to be fill. Frankie had the trucks alright but he got most of them from a subcontractor. That contractor had an agreement with the landfill that enabled him to dump.

I set up a system where each truck that left the site was logged out and we had periodic inspections. God only knows what was in those trucks and what was in that soil. I did my best. A truck held so many yards and I was paying by the yard. So when I was around the site, I climbed up on the trucks and checked. I think they might have known in advance I was coming.

My real job was to get that shit the hell out of there and I had trucks coming and going like crazy. We were doing a good hundred trucks a day up from maybe 20 and this lasted for about 40 days. Frankie was getting trucks from all over the city, with me screaming at him incessantly for more. God only knows where the drivers were coming from. Does the knowledge that less than a few years later the owner of the carting company, the guy with the license, went to jail for a long time give you any clue to what's coming? If not, how about the fact that my people were pushing the hell out of me to get the stuff out?

Turns out people from the neighborhood were calling the building department and complaining about us working without a permit. Technically, we didn't need a permit, because all we were doing was moving soil around. We were not excavating, and we were not building anything. But it didn't take long for the people in the mayor's office to connect the dots with the help of the strong arms from the neighborhood. Someone at the Department of Sanitation got wind of the fact that we were bringing the material to the Staten Island land fill. What was wrong with any of this? We got a stop work order. How could this even be? Stop what work, we were legally dumping and paying through the nose for the privilege.

All around me people were having shit fits. Out of nowhere we were being asked to test the soil. Why? The truth is no one really knew what was in that soil, whatever tests we may have had. But we knew where it came from. It was the products of dredging that was done in the Hudson River to build the Twin Towers. For some reason, the fancy lawyers just quit on us and I think it was because we were trying to push through some emergency testing and they wanted us to stop the operation and engage in a full out testing protocol. Again, why was the soil even subject to testing?

Because that mother fucking son of a bitch was using it as cover! I use the exact same words here that I used on Frankie. But it wasn't him. All he was doing was scrambling to get me trucks and loading them with his own equipment. He made money on the job, but I don't think he was making enough to screw Donald – or me. Or maybe he felt he had might on his side by virtue of the scary carter.

I had never met the guy that had the contract with the dump. I knew he existed. The day I found out that he was selling our soil for cover, I demanded to meet him. I was warned by HRH, whom I confided in, to just forget about it. No fucking way, I insisted.

The next morning I drove to a hill in the Fresh Kills landfill. I pulled up my red BMW behind a long black Mercedes. He got out, I got out. It was like a scene from a movie. The hill of garbage was shrouded in clouds of fog. The road we stood on was made out of materials he may well have supplied and the cover was our soil. It was just him and me. I started screaming from the minute I got out of my car. I called him names I would not print here. I told him if that soil came back dirty I would crush him. I don't even know half of what I told him, I was on another planet. He just told me he had no contract with me and didn't do anything wrong and he didn't like the way I was talking to him. It was totally surreal. I was totally crazy to reach out for this guy, I put myself in great jeopardy that day.

In retrospect, I don't know what I could have done differently. Mostly I was letting off steam. This guy took my material that was only good for fill and sold it for cover. What was I going to do? Sue Frankie? Meanwhile, who wanted to cast a spotlight on what could be seen as, in a very forgiving light, as a clandestine operation. All the swells around me thought this soil was dirty as hell. Donald, his brother Robert, our hotshot Director of Development and Donald's inside lawyer. And we all suffered through the testing which was done by a reputable company. I think that the environmental lawyers had convinced themselves that they had no part of this dredge spoil waste and once it fell under scrutiny, they had to quit.

But, somehow the material was clean. I do not and will not ever know what really happened here. I know that I walked on that soil with the same shoes that I walked on the rugs at home that my 2 year olds crawled on. That Robert and Harvey and Tony thought that this was severely contaminated shit and didn't warn me, putting me in potential danger, is amazing. It's funny because I remember that when I started the operation, the group went down to the site to see what we were doing and Robert told me he thought the men operating the heavy equipment should be wearing masks. The truth is if they told me that the soil was no good, they knew I would not have supervised its removal.

I always put the project first, sometimes to my own detriment. Confronting that contractor like that was probably the stupidest move I made in my professional career. This was the kind of guy who could have you killed and make it look like an accident. That he ended up in jail for a long time, only makes me shiver. He probably laughed me off as a "stupid broad" and that's what saved me. I can say with certainty that my valor was not appreciated or even recognized. But, I have learned well that you seek recognition within yourself and that is your reward. In this case, I smack myself upside the head and say, "don't ever do that again."

Chapter 12 - THE PLAZA

Donald coveted the Plaza Hotel for as long as I can remember. You could see the 1907 Beaux Arts building from the window in his office in Trump Tower and it just seemed to call out to him. Donald insisted he would someday own it. In July, 1988, Donald finally bought the Plaza. One of the first things he did was to put Ivana in charge of running the hotel. She had been working in Atlantic City for a good time, spending most of her weekdays there. Some people say she was in charge, some say she was in the way. I tend to think based on my knowledge and experience, it was a little of both.

There was already a general manager in place at the Plaza. If Donald thought he needed a better one, all he had to do was put the word out. In those days, people lined up outside the around the block for a chance to work for "The Donald". Why put Ivana in charge of this $400 million investment, just like that? Well, one answer is that if Donald thinks someone can do a job, he will not stand on ceremony. He couldn't care less about a degree in hotel management from Cornell. (Besides they say that is not the same as a BA in Literature or a BS in Chemistry – the hotel school is there for rich kids to be able to get a Cornell diploma.) Ivana did not necessarily have the credentials to be in charge of one of the most important hotels in New York, but what the hell? If Donald really believed that Ivana was actually running, and doing an excellent job at it, with the hotel in Atlantic City, why not give her a shot at the Plaza? That is definitely something that

Donald would do. But - that is not the way it went down.

Unfortunately, there is another theory that makes a bit more sense. There was a man named Steve Hyde who was really running the Atlantic City Trump Empire, and a man named Mark Etess, who was in charge of the Taj Mahal project. So, if one believes that Ivana was really only overseeing fabric selection and the like, at the casino, then making her the Manager of a very major hotel in New York might not pass the smell test. Of course, she had a real sense of style and had studied decorating and learned a hell of a lot since her days at the Grand Hyatt, and after all, there was a competent staff in place at the Plaza – why not just park her there as a figure head and let her supervise the interior design for the planned renovation? But why the need to "park" Ivana anywhere? Well, rumor had it that Donald was heavily involved in "L'Affaire" with a certain Miss Marla Maples, and he was planning to install Marla in Atlantic City, and certainly *not* under Ivana's watchful eye. I am afraid this theory may be closer to the truth. Atlantic City was the love nest and the Plaza was the ultimate vanity boost that would keep Ivana distracted. We'll never know. But when the tragic helicopter crash killed Hyde and Etess in the fall of 1989, there was never any talk of sending Ivana back to Atlantic City.

In the early summer of 1988, Ivana was installed as President of the Plaza Hotel. Not long after, the renovation talks began. I was involved at first and then somehow I managed to extricate myself. I was, after all, working on the design of two major shopping centers, and helping with the West Side project. By the end of 1988, I was back in charge of a multi-million dollar restoration project at the Plaza Hotel which would take the entire year to complete.

    Over the year 1989, the Trumps went from being *the* New York or American or even International Power Couple to the divorce scandale of the decade, (although that news would not break for a few months.) But for me, 1989 was one of my best years ever, working wise, physically, emotionally and financially. And the Plaza had a lot to do with it.

    I had a wonderful office at Trump Tower, but once I started really putting time in at the Plaza, I decided I needed to have some kind of a home there too. So the General Manager, Dick Wilhelm, took one of the rooms out of service and gave it to me to use as an office. I have to laugh at the concept that they would ever sell this room, it was tiny. It was called a single. It should have been called a small single cell. There was just enough room for two desks, mine and my secretary Cecelia's. You couldn't hold a meeting in the room with more than 3 people because that is the most who could stand up at one time. It didn't last long. Within a few weeks, I was installed in a two bedroom suite. This was more like it. I had my own office, a room for plans and a plan table, and the living room was a reception area where my secretary sat and kept the files. Living in a room like that was a terrific idea because it gave me tremendous insight into the condition of the building and also the way the old style rooms could be reworked as modern hotel rooms. We were renovating a lot of rooms, creating new suites and upgrading all of the public spaces, except for the restaurants. We did however redo the ceiling in the Palm Court which was an incredible accomplishment, given we only had to close it down for a couple of days, and the success of that venture goes, in large part, to the creativity of Ivana Trump.

    In order to fix that ceiling, we would have to scaffold the entire restaurant. Scaffolds are planked platforms that stand on closely spaced metal supports. None of this is pretty. We were perfectly capable of coming up with the materials, wood, metal brackets, screws, but there was nothing we could do to eliminate the effect. The Palm Court was one of the most popular features of the hotel and making money. The thought of closing it off, or worse, keeping it open during construction was catastrophic.

    Ivana came up with an idea that was nothing less than brilliant. First we painted everything white. Next, she found this beautiful silk material (it might have been rayon, but it looked like silk) the color of the greenest leaves. We draped the fabric around all of the steel members, and hung it from the scaffold above along with a white tulle fabric, which sat under the painted planking. Finally we returned the palms and plants to the main room. Instead of a big negative driving the crowds away, it was so inventive that people actually came to see it. The customer was cleverly invited to be part of the restoration of the great hotel, and to watch it from the inside.

That was the Trump way - turning sows ears into silk purses on a regular basis. Trump was *so* the master of publicity that you never knew where he ended and the agencies began. It was Donald who got people talking, and Ivana too. When Trump bought the Plaza, everyone expected great things to follow. This hotel which was iconic in New York City history had fallen upon hard times and showed its age more than it reflected its incredible history. Donald was expected to restore the Plaza to its proper place.

Trump hired a restoration architect who actually worked in the building, Lee Pomeroy and Associates, to do most of the design. He also brought in the venerable Hugh Hardy of Hardy Holtzman Pfeiffer because the Plaza was a Landmark and the city had very strict rules about what you can do with a landmark, especially the exterior. There was an attic at the Plaza. There were little windows in the green patinized copper mansard roof. Donald wanted to extend that space and create million dollar condos up there. This would be a massive undertaking, landmarks wise, and Donald needed the heaviest artillery available. At the time, that was Hugh Hardy. Plus, he wanted to co-opt Hardy from being part of the opposition. So it worked both ways for Donald.

We were rebuilding everything at once. Donald had already arranged to have the outside spruced up. The torchieres which are these beautiful multi armed light fixtures which graced the two entrances to the hotel were once brass but had been painted over many times with black paint. These were stripped and covered in gold leaf.

    The plan was to renovate the public spaces and to do that the first thing required was new carpeting. Although there was an incredible mosaic tile floor in many parts of the hotel, it had been covered with wall to wall for years. Lee Pomeroy did his best to encourage Donald to restore it, but he could have stood on his head, Donald was going with carpet. I do not think the Trumps, or Donald, at least, appreciated the beauty of the tile. He would eventually restore it in the Main Lobby, because a movie company wanted to use the hotel and they paid to do it. Subsequently, Donald loved it. But he knew what was there when Ivana had carpeting made to order in India to cover it up, he just cheaped it out. Ultimately, nothing was more important than money.

    Another bone of contention with the architect was the ceiling in the Fifth Avenue Lobby. There was a beautiful decorative ceiling in there that had been covered over with ductwork and electric lights in the 1950s. A plain dropped sheetrock ceiling had been hung underneath. Pomeroy wanted to restore the original ceiling but that would have involved moving all the mechanical work at great cost. Again, Donald did not see the benefit of restoring the ceiling, when he could have us install a decorative one on top of the sheetrock, which we did. There were balconies fronting on the lobby, some mirrored and some with real glass doors. It was quite decorative as it was and very beautiful when we finished it. A restoration would have been a colossal waste of money and time, and underappreciated.

    I can understand what Pomeroy wanted to do, but sometimes it was really unreasonable. For instance, the Palm Court ceiling was originally a beautiful decorative iron and stained glass ceiling that had been abandoned in the 40s or 50s when Hilton took over the hotel. It was replaced with a decorative glass paneled ceiling which was now in disrepair. Pomeroy wanted us to restore the original ceiling. This would have been a huge undertaking. Instead, we repaired what was there, added moldings, gold leafed them, repaired the decorative coffer work, etc. and ended up with a spectacular finish. Many years later, new owners spent a small fortune on a condo conversion for the Plaza and they restored that ceiling. They also closed the hotel for 5 years. We did not close the hotel for even a day.

    Donald could be very finicky about the work he did do though, and sometimes he actually wasted money. There was a magnificent wood railing on the balcony that ran along the side of the Grand Ballroom. My guess it had been painted 50 times. Donald wanted us to remove the paint. We tried stripping, spraying and sandblasting but the finish was not smooth enough for him. Of course, throughout this, there was a lot of Donald screaming at me, telling me it looks like shit. Anyway, we ended up melting the paint off with high output dryers. Yes he got a perfect finish when we repainted but the cost was just ridiculous.

Working with Donald and Ivana was like standing in center court during a training match between the Williams sisters. The shots came fast and furious and often times I got hit. She would want one color, he would tell me do another color. She was up, he was down. I think Donald resented Ivana's success at the Plaza. We had our own in-house decorating group that Ivana had been working with since the days of the first Atlantic City Hotel. The designer was very talented and he and Ivana were like two peas in a pod. Unfortunately, he died right before we started the Plaza. Ivana was personally devastated, and left with only the assistant decorator, who was OK, and a talented young architect who had worked on the Princess in Atlantic City.

Here's how it would work. Ivana would pull pictures out of magazines of things she liked and give them to her designers. Mostly it was stuff from castles in Europe or Newport mansions, but they did their best to copy them and pulled it off with knockoffs, copies and reproductions. In some ways it sounds very amateurish, but it worked, at least to the extent that they wanted and sufficiently to make Donald jealous. Ivana was the president of the hotel, Dick Wilhelm the general manager and I was in charge of the renovation. Ivana and her team got the job done and she was receiving recognition right and left. It was obvious to me that Donald didn't expect this, but screw him. What was he thinking when he put Ivana in charge and gave her me to do the work? That we would fail?

I was number three in the pecking order at the hotel and that came with terrific perks. It took a long time for me to realize that I could eat in any of the restaurants for free, although I didn't do that very much. I loved the food at the Plaza, but mostly I brought along a contractor who paid for the meal. It was good for business.

I got very friendly with the chef, who Ivana had purloined from a famous French restaurant in New York, called Le Cirque. His name was Alain. He had been complaining about a number of problems and his complaints fell on deaf ears until I took over the management of the renovation. One of the first things I got done for Alain was the installation of air conditioning in the waiters waiting area. Ivana had purchased new wool uniforms for the room service waiters. Kitchens are kept hot because that is the way chefs usually like them, but the room service guys were dying in their area with their hot clothes, the result of which was smelly guys bringing food up to the rooms and complaining to the Chef. This was easily solved but it took someone with the clout to make the argument for it with Donald and the ability to make it happen.

At first, the extent of the "restoration" was just going to be renovation of some rooms, mostly decorating level work, and I had tapped this very talented young man who had worked for me at Trump Tower, David Dods, to be the onsite project manager. But we soon got very involved and I needed to be there more, if for nothing else than to balance out the power. So David and I were the construction people and we did everything together. I also ran interference with the Trumps and made his life a bit easier.

Since the chef came to me whenever he had a problem and I always solved it, he was very good to me. I liked the Edwardian Room and I ate there fairly often. There was a table at the corner of 59th and 5th, it overlooked the Grand Army Plaza. When Donald ate at the Plaza, he sat there. When he wasn't there, it was mine. The Plaza days were good for the ego. Whomever I was with, I was met by the Maitre D', another pal, escorted to my table, and after the food came out, Chef Alain always showed up at the table to see if everything was up to snuff. I was treated the same way at the Oak Room and the Fish Restaurant, where the chef there would prepare special meals just for me. These were all very nice people. I was someone they could actually talk to, who would listen, which gave them a real voice and they were excited about what the Trumps were doing. So everyone was basically happy in 1989, the year I did most of my work.

We had a banquet manager who was an aristocratic old school kind of guy and his head assistant, Paul Nicaj, who was a character – Western European with an accent, cute in his own way and very efficient. Of course, you checked your pockets when you left him. He was a conniver – a "by hook or by crook" kind of guy, but I loved him. He was basically in charge of all the banquets. I was renovating all of the public spaces so we had to work together to make sure that rooms would be available when he booked them. If he had a problem he came to me, and that worked out great with Ivana and Wilhelm because they wanted me to solve the problems without having to go through a whole rigmarole. That is the beauty of private work, and working with owners who trust you. The Trumps trusted me. Of course, they also got to blame me when they made mistakes. Part of the job.

Paul was a friend, and as I said, a cut up. In June of that year, my nephew was graduating from Tenafly High School and they had their prom at the Plaza. I gave Paul Victor's name and asked him to do something special. Forget about it. Paul brought his table champagne among other things. I don't know how he got away with this, but Victor was a rock star that night.

Like I said, Paul was crafty. Without consulting me, he had booked a tremendous bar mitzvah in one of the larger ballrooms which we had not touched yet, and that was fine. Just adjacent to it was a smaller room that I had already torn apart. It had partial ceiling, no paint, walls with holes in them, no light fixtures, and the old wood floor which was in bad shape and covered with water stains and paint. Inside the room was a full scaffold with men installing the ceiling which was to be a very decorative ceiling with special plaster molds that we had purchased in Canada. This room was scheduled to be finished in about a month, but Paul promised the mother who was arranging the ceremonies that we would have it finished in time for her to use it as an adjunct to the party so the young teens could congregate in there. I didn't see the contract, but my guess is that if the room hadn't been finished, they could have accomplished what she needed right there in a corner of the big ballroom which was humongous, but Paul promised her this room. Paul rolled the dice, figuring he could count on me. He had a fallback position.

I think I found out about the Bar Mitzvah about three or four days before it was to happen. On Thursday, two days before the party, the room was still full of scaffold and it looked like nothing had been done at all. I got an emergency call from Paul on my walkie talkie to meet him down there. I went down to the room to find Paul outside with a woman he was hugging who was sobbing. Paul said please tell Mrs. So and so that the room will be ready Saturday.

Here's something about completion dates. You will them to happen. As with the Trump Tower opening, anyone who was not in the thick of it, and knowledgeable about construction, would have taken a look at that room and laughed, or cried, as the case at hand. I was worried but I had the will to finish and I would keep the men there around the clock if needed. So I assured the woman and Paul was happy. We did work almost around the clock. The under ceiling was finished, most of the outside molding was on and we had hi-hats in the ceiling. I had the walls painted white on white, and I got a light pink wall to wall carpet and installed it on the floor. When it was finished it looked nice. When I went back Saturday afternoon, I found the room had been filled with pinball machines and other games, a popcorn maker, soda dispensers. It was spectacular - a kid's paradise! Paul came in with the mother and she was ecstatic. She couldn't thank me enough. I later learned from Paul that he got an extraordinary gratuity that day. We both had our rewards. This was a nice thing.

You do not finish construction jobs without a deadline. So even if you have to make one up, you have to have that "must finish by" date. This was the case with the Presidential Suite at the Plaza Hotel. The Presidential Suite was a mess to put it mildly. I do not think it had been updated since the 60s and it was really cheap and worn. But as they say, the bones were great. We pretty much gutted the whole thing and started over, preserving most of the rooms, but pulling out all the fixtures, wall treatments (like the basement style wall paneling), the entire kitchen, and all the built-ins and started from scratch. We reconfigured some walls to make the rooms more modern. It was a beautiful space. But we needed a date to push the finish, or we would get stalled, and something came up that filled the bill.

Elton John was going to be in New York for a concert at Madison Square Garden. So we started the rumor that the suite had to be finished for Elton John to occupy. We pushed hard to get that work done, it was asses and elbows all the way. Unfortunately, the finishes were horrible and the suite came out terribly, we all thought. There was so much red. And large prints. And of course, gold leaf everywhere. The word is gaudy. Another word is horrible. Anyway, we got it finished in time for Elton John *not* to stay there, because he never was going to. I stayed there one night though. I am not sure if they ever rented the whole suite, at a $10,000/night rate, but I know they did rent out parts of it. It was dividable. It is a fantastic space, it was just too over the top decorating wise. A rare stumble for Ivana.

Ivana was much more subtle in the other rooms and they came out just great. She redid all of the meeting rooms and small ballrooms. People liked them. These small meeting rooms were used for photo shoots and commercials by high fashion people all the time.

Right around the time Donald bought the Plaza, a Werner LeRoi restaurant called the Potomac was closing in bankruptcy in Washington, DC. All the furniture, fixtures and equipment was for sale. LeRoi, known for his "Crystal Room" at The Tavern on The Green in Central Park, decorated his restaurants with colorful Austrian crystal chandeliers. Ivana bought the used chandeliers from the Potomac and brought them to the Plaza, and designed the meeting rooms around them. We had a blue room, a green room, a red room and a gold room, each picking up the colors of the crystals. Ivana also had copies made of French murals painted by an artist named Fragonard. These were copies but they were still very expensive. We made picture frames on the walls with moldings, and glued the murals inside. The rooms they were in were known as the Fragonard suites. No walls were plain, no ceilings, no doors – it was all about moldings, wood and plaster and lots of gold at the Plaza.

Donald was fond of his gold and it was all over the Plaza. Of course, Ivana was fond of it too. But while we used real gold in Trump Tower, everything in the Plaza was made of something call Dutch metal or imitation gold leaf which was about 5% of the cost of gold. Dutch metal is really brass in sheets like leaf and gets applied the same way. But Donald said it was gold and people believed it. He cheaped out a lot of things and got away with it.

We redid the pre-function room outside the main ballroom and restored the ceiling to the original design. No scrimping there or in the powder rooms, which were fabulous – lots of pink marble. We restored the Main Ballroom and the Terrace Room. As of today, they remain relatively intact.

In November, Ivana held the March of Dimes Gourmet Gala in the Terrace Room. This was Ivana's event and an indicative of her new status in Society. Ivana was now Ivana Trump, as opposed to Mrs. Donald Trump. To the world, the Trumps were even more the "golden couple" and Donald cooked hamburgers at Ivana's charity event just like any other celebrity, Mike Tyson or Barbara Walters. But there were things going on behind the scenes. For months we executives had been hearing rumors about a blonde. I remember there was a big sporting event, I didn't go, but one of the women in the office, who did, came back and told me about a woman who was seated in the audience fairly close to Donald. Donald had gone with a close business associate, whom my friend referred to as "the beard". It was the first time that

I had ever heard this expression. I learned that there had been several occasions of "the blonde" showing up to things that Donald had attended, ostensibly with business associates.

Then there was the boat. In 1988, Donald bought the Nabila, the largest privately owned yacht in the world at the time, from Adnan Kashoggi, the arms dealer, for $30 million or so. He put about $8 million more into it, and annexed it to the Princess Casino for the high rollers, and it seems, Marla Maples as well. Wherever she might have been holed up, Marla was very big part of Donald's life by the end of 1989.

The truth came out, as it were, in February 1990, but in the late fall of 1989, neither Donald nor Ivana seemed to be in very good moods. We were finishing up guest rooms and Donald came over to look at the work. The rooms had just been redecorated and refurnished and I was finishing up the new bathrooms. Donald did the walk through with me the decorator and the assistant general manager. He wasn't happy. He wasn't happy long before he even walked into the building. Ivana had bought new armoires for the TV sets. She was insistent that the doors retracted into the units instead of opening out to the side, so opening and closing the doors took a little bit of care. We had them custom made to her specifications. Donald said that the armoires were shit, and he got so mad, he pulled the door off one of the units cursing, "fucking Ivana, this is fucking crap, it's garbage", that sort of thing. Then we went into the bathroom. I was installing green marble on the floor. It was a Chinese stand in for a Vermont marble called antique verde, but it was no match, and we knew it. I used that marble, with Donald's blessing, because it was a third the cost of the real thing. Donald took one look at this marble and started screaming at me. He was shaking. "You did this," he said. "You bought this cheap shit and now you are making me look like a jerk. You're no fucking good." I said, "Look Donald, this is the marble you approved. It was cheap, you wanted to save money. Don't blame me." It was like pouring gasoline on a fire. His face was red. His mouth was all twisted and I thought to myself, if he hits you, just take a fall. He was so angry, I thought he might hit me. Of course, he wouldn't.

But it wasn't me he was really mad at. He was mad at his life. He already knew his marriage was over, and my gut tells me he knew that he had other problems as well. Whatever the reason, he was crazed this day. I don't know if he realized I was right, or decided that he had to get himself under control, but he walked out of the room and we went to another room to look at. Now *I* was shaking. He directed his anger at the furniture and the decorator and left me alone after that. Word about the incident spread quickly and I became a bit of a legend at the Plaza for standing up to Donald.

In early January, not long after the marble incident, I ran into an acquaintance of mine at Trump Tower. Billy was a developer/contractor in a family business who, in his young life, had accomplished much and traveled in circles where he would come into contact with Donald. He wanted very much to work for Donald and had written and called him many times. Donald was Billy's idol. I tried to find out what he was doing there, but he was quite vague. I smelled a rat. I had been on the outs with Donald for a while and I was thinking, maybe he is bringing Billy in to replace me.

I went over to the Plaza where I had been heading when I encountered Billy. I took care of my business there and then I went to see Ivana in her office. She didn't look too good. I said to her, "Ivana, I think Donald may be thinking about firing me." To my utter surprise, she started to cry. She said, "You don't know what it's like. You only work with him, you're only around him in the daytime. I am with him twenty four hours a day." I was flabbergasted. I had come in to say goodbye. I was fond of Ivana and I was pretty sure I was on the way out. I wanted to talk to her, and tell her how I felt about her, and that I knew it had nothing to do with her and that Donald was crazy. This was like walking into a land mine. I always knew Donald gave her a hard time. Plus I had heard the rumors about the blonde. So, it made sense that she wasn't in the best of moods, but I wasn't prepared for *this*! She went on to say that no matter what happened, I would be okay. She said I was strong. She went off on a stream of consciousness about how alike we were and ended up saying she thought the world of me and promising to give me the best recommendation. We talked a bit and I thanked her. I felt really bad when I left. I thought to myself, yeah, she's right, I *can* walk away from him.

I headed back to the office to confront Donald. When I finally met him with him, I asked him if he had a problem with my work. I had already confirmed my suspicions. Billy had been nosing around and talking to people. Donald said no, and I asked him why Billy was involved, and Donald just said Billy wanted a job so he sent him over to the Plaza to take a look at what we were doing there. This was pure unadulterated bullshit. If that were so, he would have asked me to take Billy over there, not go behind my back. Plus, I had an assistant at the Plaza, an architect named David Dods, who was doing a great job over there. I did not need anyone else. Donald basically shooed me out of his office, and I never heard a thing from Donald about Billy until he hired him months later. Billy eventually worked for me on the West Side Yards. He is still a good friend. My associate, who had told me about "the beard", gave me the scoop on Billy. For some reason or another Donald thought something was going on at the Plaza and when Billy came onto the screen, Donald decided to send him over to check it out. Billy came back with what my friend called "glowing reports." To this day, I do not know what would have motivated Donald to do this. My friend thinks it may have had something to do with what was going on between Donald and Ivana, and he wanted to know where I stood. Who knows?

Unfortunately, when the scandal broke in February, we did have to choose sides and, of course, I had to go with Donald. But I had been through a lot with Ivana and I knew she was suffering. People said she was cold but that is not at all the case. I knew Ivana when and she was a very warm caring person. She was hardened by Donald, like I was hardened by the business basic survival. Then she became famous, the fame went a little bit to her head like it does with mostly everyone else who achieves it.

I knew the story before the news broke. Again from my associate in the office. The Trumps always went to Aspen over the Christmas vacation. This time Donald had brought his girlfriend, Marla Maples, with him. Ivana found out and there was a big confrontation. By the time she broke down in her office when I went to tell her goodbye, this already had happened and Ivana knew her marriage was over. I don't know if Ivana ever cheated on Donald but I would be surprised if she had the time. She worked all the time and took care of her family which she adored. Plus she was at Donald's side for countless black tie dinners and ribbon cuttings, she never said no to anything, and I doubt she ever said no to him.

In the spring of 1989, Spy Magazine had run a horrible article about Ivana and put her on the cover in a picture that made her look awful – pruny and not pretty. In fact, Ivana was gorgeous. But she must have felt like she needed it, because she went soon after and had a lot of plastic surgery done. She later said that she had done the work to try to hold on to Donald. When she healed she was like a younger version of her gorgeous self. Apparently it was not enough. So it was this new improved Ivana that cried bitterly in January 1990 in her office in front of me. Ivana did not deserve this.

We were pretty much finished in the Plaza and I had a new assignment to worry about. Donald had joined with European partners to develop the former Ambassador Hotel in Los Angeles where he would build a 6 million square foot mixed use hotel office apartment shopping and entertainment extravaganza. In January, we had all gone to LA, the partners, Donald and Ivana, too, to announce the partnership, meet the mayor and unveil our plans to the Press. Looking back at this I think it must have been hell for Ivana. But she was game, and very brave. In the end, Ivana was a survivor and continues to do herself proud.

Donald ended up disbanding Ivana's decorating office and let the three people working there go. I grabbed up Steve Lawler, a very classy guy who was a real architect and knew a lot about construction, to be my Project Manager on the Ambassador job, and the next time I would go to the Plaza for any reason was to attend the wedding of Donald Trump and Marla Maples, the blonde.

Chapter 13 Two Failures

In the spring of 1989, Donald asked me to go to California to evaluate a project for him. I was smart enough to understand that if he was really interested in this, he would have sent Harvey and Robert, but I dutifully winged out to LA to meet a man known as David Schein who had an interest in the just closing Ambassador Hotel. I looked at the project with David. It was a very famous hotel in a very run down area of Los Angeles, with enough property to build several million square feet of something, but under the circumstances, what that was escaped me. Schein took me home to his Mansion to meet his former beauty queen wife and his family took me to dinner before I grabbed the red-eye back to New York. He was terrific and the hotel was interesting but I didn't see anything for us there. I reported my findings to Donald and went back to work on my other projects.

Several months later, one of Donald's closest advisors, a lawyer named Jerry Shrager, brought in a group of primarily European investors who had just purchased the Ambassador Hotel, and were interested in bringing Donald in as a partner to do a massive development there. This group had just bought a major building in New York and had done a small, but very successful, retail development in Beverly Hills. They looked like they had the right experience and they certainly had the money. They were willing to take Donald in for 20%. He would have to pay his way in, but they were going to give him all his expenses and a big fee on the work he did to develop the project, then real estate fees on sales and leasing. This looked like a win win for DJT because once he paid the purchase price, the other costs would be covered. Donald signed on the dotted line and put me in charge of the project.

The Ambassador, although closed, was a thriving movie set rental business. There was a staff of former employees who had remained to manage the property while its new owners decided its fate and also to handle the leasing. The company also owned several small apartment buildings on the property which needed to be taken care of and we had a car rental tenant and a couple of billboards. The income was not enough to pay the taxes but it did pay the salaries of all the people that the owners kept around - a payroll clerk, a secretary, some groundskeepers and guards.

We were aware that the local school board, the Los Angeles Unified School District, had its eyes on the property as a potential school site. We also realized that it was way too expensive and we had a realtor working on finding alternate sites for them so they would leave us alone. The LAUSD is a disproportionately powerful entity, given its track record of abject incompetence, and capable of making anyone's life miserable because it had the ability to use eminent domain. Eminent Domain is in the 5th Amendment of the Constitution. It says the government can take you property if it needs it. The landowner's protection is that they will get a fair price. But if you are only threatened with condemnation, you are stopped dead in your tracks and at the mercy of the threatening agency. This can cost a property owner millions in planning costs and lost opportunities and usually they rush to make a deal. Legal blackmail is what it is. In our case, we did not take the LAUSD seriously and that was a mistake. The school board have never paid anything like what we paid for the Ambassador for a school site, and did not have the money available to buy it, anyway.

My job was to find an architect and put a team together to build a Trump styled project in Los Angeles. Naturally, it would include the world's tallest building. One of the first things we did was schedule a press conference. I wrote the press release. I still barf over it. The project would be called Trump City. Something about bringing the future to the city of the future. Mayor Bradley and Councilman Nate Holden came to the conference along with the local Wilshire Center Developers and Tenants groups. Everyone wanted us there because we would revitalize the area. This was the place where the original Oscars ceremony was held. The famous and closed Brown Derby restaurant was across the street. Thousands of movie stars slept in our beds, lived in our cottages. Mid Wilshire was once a mecca! If anyone in the world could save the community it was Donald Trump.

We interviewed several big name architects and decided to go with a mid-sized firm called Johnson Fain Pereira. Donald really liked the two young architects that ran the firm and they had the chops to do a project like this. Plus they were local and that was a big thing for us. We didn't want to come in with a Skidmore or some other out of town group. We were going to try to look like we belonged. I put together the rest of the team with Structural Engineers, Mechanical Engineers etc. The partners, formerly known as Wilshire Center Partners, until we changed the name to Trump Wilshire Associates, had hired the very best land use lawyer, and also had a lobbying firm and public relations in place and they were all top notch. We had a terrific team and, before long, we would have a terrific project. I had already met with the city planning people and the Mayor of course was promoting us. There was no question we would be a shoe in. The plan was going to be a massive shopping center, topped with an office building, on top of that a super luxury hotel and then apartments. All together, we would be doing 6 million square feet. Donald was talking to the owner of Harrad's about creating a version of the London store at our site. The only problem was LAUSD was still saber rattling and no matter what we proposed to them, they wanted the Ambassador site.

LAUSD suggested we do a joint building that is part commercial and part school. I did my research to prove how this concept had failed in cities like New York. Meanwhile, the local businesses and politicians were putting pressure on LAUSD to go elsewhere. And we had found several sites for them and had spent the money drawing potential schools on these sites. LAUSD made up reasons not to accept our suggestions.

We officially started the project in early January with the press conference. By the end of June, the LAUSD had voted to condemn the project. They pulled a few strings and got a bond issue approved for purposes other than to take our property and decided they would only condemn a portion of the piece, so the bond funds were adequate to cover what they were condemning and, in one fell swoop, took away our ability to do anything with that property except wait. The ensuing six plus years of hell is fodder for a book of its own. Suffice it to say here that it was in California, courtesy of the Los Angeles Unified School District, that I learned to lobby. I also learned a lot about the law, attended probably 500 hours of depositions, vetted thousands of documents, appeared before state boards, two mayors, countless aides, several agencies, testified for 12 days in court, appeared in countless interviews in print and on TV and learned more about condemnation that I needed to know and more about bureaucracy, greed, malevolence, corruption and incompetency that I ever wanted to learn. It took almost 40 years for LAUSD to build a single high school, and when it opened it school on the Ambassador site in 2011, it was the most expensive school by a wide margin on the face of the earth. Delivered to you by perjurers, thieves and fools.

When we realized that we would not be able to do anything with the Ambassador, Donald called me in for a pep talk. This was one of the most sincere and human conversations I ever had with him. He told me he understood that I was probably depressed, that he would be too, and that I needed to wait it out and new things will come up and I will get over it. I had missed a lot while I was out in Los Angeles. For one thing, Trump opened the Taj Mahal, an opening I would have attended, as I had the Trump Plaza, if it weren't for a meeting of the California State Allocation Board that I was speaking at.

The Taj was an amazing place, and although I never stayed there, I certainly visited it. I had come in to New York and brought along the City Council Member who represented the Wilshire Center district. He was coming up to Sacramento with me to lobby the state to turn down the school district's requests for funds to put a school at the Ambassador site. Donald was running from place to place and he wanted to take a meeting with Councilman Holden, but the only place he had the time to give him would be on a trip to Atlantic City. So Donald invited Nate Holden to accompany him on a helicopter ride to AC with me, his brother and Harvey Freeman. Donald regularly rented small helicopters and he had larger black ones with his name in red that he used to shuttle high rollers. Our helicopter was beige and it had two pilots. It was quite luxurious, I had been in a similar one a few times.

As we pulled out over the Hudson, the helicopter began to shake. We were at the convergence of the Hudson River and the Long

Island Sound and Harvey explained that where the ocean water meets the fresh river water, certain air currents arise that cause disturbances. From the corner of my eye, I can see in the cockpit and what I see is the co-pilot pumping a device with all his might. I am thinking Harvey is full of shit as Donald and Robert are reassuring Nate. Very shortly thereafter the pilot let us know he had lost some instruments and we would need to make an emergency landing. By now, the helicopter was shaking like crazy. Donald loves to tell the story that Nate, an African American, turned white, but as I recall Donald was pretty white himself, and the others looked none too comfortable. Some time earlier, Donald had lost three executives in a helicopter crash and they were all scared shitless, as was I. We landed in New Jersey at an airport where Donald had his commuter helicopters stored. Within an hour we were safely in Atlantic City, Nate and I had a nice lunch courtesy of Donald and went back to New York. We may not have gotten much business done, but it sure as hell was memorable.

Nate was in our corner, regardless, and truth be told, it didn't make a damned bit of difference. Mayor Bradley sent his number one aide to Sacramento and Holden came in person and we had the support of the state Assemblyman, and we had the facts and the law on our side and none of it mattered. The allocation was voted down. Two minutes later, Assemblywoman Maxine Waters came flying into the room, fresh from the ways and means committee which she chaired. She had a word with the member of the committee representing the General Services Commission who had just voted down the allocation. Within a short minute, he called for reconsideration, a measure under Robert's Rules which allows a recently heard and voted upon motion to be voted on again. This man changed his vote and LA got the money. Plain and simple Maxine threatened him. The vote, which we had managed to lobby into a no, through a renegade Senator who we worked over for weeks, was reversed by the General Services member, who had been a guaranteed no vote - a consistent opponent against giving Los Angeles permission to squander tens of millions of dollars. This is the very first time I saw the underbelly of politics but it paled next to the antics LAUSD would pull over the next 8 years.

Another major development that happened while I was traipsing up to Sacramento was the resignation of Tony Gliedman. The West Side project was now without a leader and Donald tapped me to take over.

I had a game plan which was probably Donald's idea, but I was going to execute it. We had several major points in our favor which we were primed to exploit. For one thing, the opposition was formidable but it was local. Local to the area, to be specific and it was comprised of wealthy people. Donald always targets the common man as his ally although Donald never spent a poor day in his life. But regular guys relate to Donald and people in New York think of him as a great builder, so in this time, the number one benefit of building Trump City was jobs. Construction Jobs by the thousands and then permanent jobs. Our plan was to build 14 million square feet. Even if it got negotiated down to 10 and we fully expected to negotiate down the size, and the height for that matter, we would be bringing work to the city. Local Unions were feeling the pain of the new recession with thousands of skilled worker laid off or furloughed. My plan was a march on city hall. There was no doubt in my mind that the Construction Unions would support this.

The next thing was the nearest subway station at 72nd Street and Broadway was so ridiculously past its ability to serve the population that you were lucky to get near it at peak hours much less get on a train. We were proposing a complete redo - A whole new station that would carry the current loads plus all the predicted ridership that was generated by our development.

Another thing we had was a massive beautification plan. Parks everywhere, I mean real parks with baseball diamonds and basketball courts, something that did not necessarily sit well with the private park, trees and greens set. And the shopping center would be the first of its kind in New York, featuring all the stores that New Yorkers had to shlep out to New Jersey or Long Island to go to, which would bring millions in sales taxes to the city.

I guess, in a way, I was planning a class warfare. Calling on the 4 ½ boroughs to demand that this project get built. We were renting billboards, writing circulars, planning the marches and rallies, when Donald was approached on the QT by a "friend of a friend", who told him, "You will *never* get your plan approved." This "friend" suggested Donald take a meeting with a group of opponents to discuss a compromise position. I, of course, was opposed to this, but at the same time, our EIR was growing hairs at the Department of Environmental Protection and it was clear that the only way out for us would be litigation, which could take years. Opposed though I may have been, taking the meeting was a reasonable idea.

    The day that the meeting was held, Donald handpicked the secretaries, "girls" in the office, who would receive the guests, bring in the sandwiches and coffees, etc. Of course, he selected the four most attractive women we had. Donald didn't care what Susan, Blanche or I looked like because we were worth our looks in value, but for greeting newcomers, Donald needed to make an impression. Donald wanted the world to think that only attractive people worked for him. As a matter of fact, one day Donald was set to take a meeting with a female leader of the opposition over lunch at the Plaza. Although I had other things to do and was not necessary to the subject matter, Donald made me join him so he would not be seen sitting alone at his table with this particularly ugly woman. I got a nice meal out of it.

    The group we met with was comprised of leaders from the Coalition for a Livable West

Side, The Regional Plan, Westpride, The Municipal Arts Society, The Riverside Park Association and the National Resource Defense Council. One of these groups was made up solely by people who lived in a building whose views would be blocked if anything at all was built on our site. Another was a grassroots CAVE group (citizens against virtually everything) comprised of Donald haters, and the other four were real heavy hitters. There may have been one other. This group had plenty of money. So much money that they had hired an architect to do a plan of how to use the property in a way that they could support. At least most of them could support it. The NIMBYs (Not in MY Back Yard people), just came along for the ride and the free food, and to meet Donald in the flesh.

Their proposal required us to agree to drop the idea of any building higher than say 60 stories, and they wanted several buildings, spread out along a continuation of Riverside Park, as it were, and they should resemble famous buildings in New York like the Dakota, San Remo and the Normandy. It was a take it or leave it deal. Included in the proposition was to rename the project to Riverside South and make it a joint project, headed up by a person of the group's choosing, as well as an architect and planner, which they would also appoint.

The discussion was lengthy and went into all the ways this group could help us or hurt us. Teamed together, it was doubtless that we would get approval and our EIR would be certified. With them as opposition, it was clear that we would languish. I was not convinced. It was close to the end of the year, and we were expecting the DEP to take action at any point. We had answered all of their questions and I had been to see the head of the DEP and it looked promising. No doubt it had looked promising before. Plus we were ready to launch our new offensive and times kept getting worse for the workers. Also, our plan was superior, in that it was unique, and had much more public amenities. The plan the group brought us included only apartment buildings lined up in a row along a straight line. There was landscaping but it was limited. Included in their plan was a proposal to move the West Side Highway to below grade to slip under the development with a continuation of Riverside Park above. Of course that looked beautiful, however, I doubt anyone living or deceased ever believed that would happen, although it was a big element of the plan and everyone touted it as if it would occur in the next 20 years. Big fucking liars! In fact, thirty years later, it is no longer even being considered. The finished project is yet another enclave of the super rich, with very limited access for anyone else. Just as they wanted it.

Donald rightly agreed to the proposal. He negotiated a larger amount of square feet and a higher height for the tallest buildings, and retained some control, including the day to day management, which would remain my job, but the director of the project would be Mr. Richard Kahan, a well known lawyer developer who had done several successful projects for the city. We held a press conference with Mayor Dinkins to announce the formation of the new group and to withdraw our current plans. The head of the City Planning Commission was also present and it was all lovey dovey. Everyone was thrilled but me. I had just been put in charge of this project and now it was being wrested from me and I had no choice but to go along.

My attitude was really quite childish under the circumstances. Donald was in a very bad way. He did not have the money to pull this off. Rumors about his being bankrupt had already surfaced and soon we had a special appointee running operations for us. This man, Steve Bollenbach, was what is known as a "work out" specialist. He had a reputation for being the best in the business and he showed up to work every day in a chauffeur driven Bentley. I am sure he was brilliant at what he does, but he was not particularly sociable. I was scared to death of him. While I knew Donald would never fire me, Bollenbach could give me the ax at the drop of a dime and heads had already rolled.

We had a massive meeting with all of Donald's banks in a very large conference room in a hotel. Some of the names I recall were Citibank, Chase, Natwest, Deutchebank. There were more. I attended this meeting at the representative of the West Side Project. We went through all the possibilities of what could be done with the various properties Donald owned at the time, of which the West Side Yards was the largest. He also held his interest in the Grand Hyatt, Trump Tower, of course, the interest in the California project, and minor interests in other buildings that he had converted to condominiums, the Alexander's stock holdings and the casinos. If you added all the values of what Donald owned at the time and subtracted the amount of loans, Donald's net worth was about minus a half a billion dollars. The purpose of the meeting and subsequent deliberations was to decide what to let Donald keep and manage and what to take away. If this were a house, the bank would have just foreclosed on the property and taken what it got at a fire sale. When you're in the hole for a half a billion dollars, it takes a bit more thinking. Now you're more like a partner, than a borrower. The institutions smartly decided that most of the property was more valuable as potential development properties with the Trump brand than as empty pieces of land.

Ultimately Donald was allowed to keep his interest in Trump Tower. His Alexander's shares went to Citibank. His part of the Hyatt was sold back to Hyatt Hotels. The Casinos kept Donald's name and gave him management contracts, but he no longer owned them. As for the West Side project, Donald got a development fee. The bank group came up with the amount of money necessary to run the empire and then gave Donald that as well as a personal allowance and money to pay his alimony. Since my time was paid by the partners, the expenses for the California project were low and he held on to that too.

After attending a few meetings with Richard Kahan, I started rethinking my position. I wanted to be in charge, and with Richard heading up the project, my role was unclear. There was no question that I had the construction experience Kahan was lacking, but, still, I was uncomfortable in the role, whatever that was, and I was finding myself in between Donald and the Group. I decided it was time to bail. Donald was not happy at all with my decision. Although he had gotten rid of some people and cut other people's salaries, I was in good shape, and he could not understand why I needed to leave. At the time, my children were getting ready to start school and I had some special issues with my son, who had some motor skills issues, and when I told this to Donald he jumped on it. He said tell everybody you have to take care of your son. So that is what I did.

It wasn't so easy to let go. This had never occurred to me, but I had a great value to the group that I underestimated. Contrary to Donald's advice, I still wanted people to like me and these people liked me a lot. And they wanted me to stay. Richard Kahan and Kent Barwick took me out to lunch at fancy Restaurant. And they basically begged me to stay. And it all came into focus for me. I was running interference between Donald and the group and they wanted to keep it that way. Whatever they had to say, it was easier to say it to me. And when Donald wasn't happy, I absorbed most of the blow. In retrospect, I admit I was a fool to leave this project. My ego overrode my good sense. I did want to spend some time with my kids, but who was I fooling? I liked working 12 hour days, I liked the whirlwind of working for Trump. But he had changed. The financial woes had taken a toll on him and he was sullen and bitter. He was not the same man. I was not comfortable with him either. I walked away.

Of course, I walked away with the understanding that I would still be a consultant on the California project, and the Alexander's projects, and although Donald lost his interest in Alexander's, I didn't, and I stayed on at an hourly billing rate of $200, working for Farkas, and ultimately Steve Roth, who took over the development management position. California was billed at $240, and although the project was dead, we had a massive lawsuit ahead of us, with lots of preparation work. Between those two projects I made a good living. Bad as it looked at the time, Donald ended up doing alright too.

Chapter 14 - Transitions

When Roth took over for Donald, he had a lot of ideas, and I was just the person to help him visualize them. I spent a lot of time with him, going to Brooklyn, the Bronx, trying to figure out what the highest and best use for the various sites might be. For one thing, he wanted to kill the idea of a mall in Paramus and go with a power center there. There was a small patch of wetlands in the middle of the parking lot, which could have turned out to be a nightmare if we wanted to build anything. A large amount of the site was below the level of the flood plain and that meant that if you filled anything, you needed to locate and buy a site upon which you could create a basin to take three times the amount of water you displaced. I quickly and quietly filed the proper applications and managed to eliminate that small wetland under the approval of the Department of Environmental Protection.

Roth wanted to make friends with the people I had been suing and fighting with, and his planning was smaller scale than Donald. We contacted them and settled all the open matters, extracting a pound of flesh. Now the plan was to work together to get the Department of Transportation to clear the way for Garden State Plaza's expansion and our conversion to the Power Center Steve had in mind. The levels of service of all the nearby interchanges were at failure point and it would take a lot of new overpasses and road widenings to make this happen. However, with the both sides working together, there was no longer any opposition so the path became relatively smooth and we were free to plan what we wanted.

I had gotten a tremendous amount of Press on the Paramus project. As Trump Centre, we were on the cover of the New Jersey section of the Sunday New York Times, as well as the front page of the Sunday Record and many other papers. But this was a banner year for publicity for me, anyway. I was featured along with Susan and Blanche on the cover of Savvy Woman Magazine with a big story about the "King's women". Then there was a feature in Newsday called Inside Team Trump, which did stories about the six Executive Vice Presidents. I was interviewed in several newspapers, had a head shot in the Post and was an "Up and Coming" person to look for in Forbes Magazine. Also I did CNN and CNBC, I was having a great year.

Working with Roth was an entirely different story. He liked to keep under the radar and avoided publicity, the very opposite to what I was used to. But he was, in a sense, realer. It wasn't about just planning, spinning daydreams, promoting his name. He wanted to start working right away. Get something built and making money.

Brooklyn was his big thing. I spent a lot of time working with him on that. Alexander's had a store and owned half of the Kings Plaza Mall and that was a terrific moneymaker in need of a true renovation/remodeling. Kings Plaza had its own electrical plant, i.e., it generated the electricity used by the mall. To do this, it had several major fuel oil storage tanks and the mall had access to a navigable waterway in Mill Basin Brooklyn for deliveries. It was a very clever idea, but over time, the tanks started leaking so one of the very first things we had to do was clean up that mess. Roth wanted to bring the mall up to date and we studied several revitalization plans with a general contractor. There was so much going on with Alexander's that if you looked in any direction, another problem or proposal would pop up and attention would be diverted to the next place. The Alexander's in Green Acres had a parking lot with a steel problem. That needed to be fixed. We needed to figure out what to do with the store in the World Trade Center. Yes, Alexander's has a big presence there too. It wasn't a mall store, but it was tens of thousands of square feet of choice retail. Then we had the Bronx, another of his favorites. I think Steve had some personal connection with the Bronx. On Fordham Road, this was another killer retail location. I was in that building assessing its structural condition, and looking at ways to do a vertical mall. Steve kept me very busy.

In California, we were pursuing the condemnation action. The way condemnation works is the agency condemns the property it wants and makes an offer. You can accept the offer or sue for the amount of money you think it is actually worth. The agency puts up the money but, at least in California, they don't have to physically take the property, so you are stuck paying the taxes and keeping it operational with no hope of ever developing it while you spend a fortune in court trying to get a fair price. It is really complicated and manipulated unfairly. The district decided to take only a portion of our property so they valued that at $47 million, posted the money from the bond issue (Certificates of Participation) and prepared for war. They did not take the property. This was a tactical decision on the part of the school board. They didn't need the property at the time so why relieve us of the pressure of having to pay the taxes and upkeep. We managed to get some money in from the rentals, but overall the property operated at a large net loss and we were bleeding.

I had hired a lawyer to work on the condemnation issues from the very start. The advice he gave us was that the school district, although normally allowed to reverse its decision to condemn in California, (different from New York and New Jersey) would not be able to abandon its decision here because of the circumstances. The only use of the project was for it to be knocked down and redeveloped. This was our big selling point with the state government. We were arguing about the value of the land, and we claimed that at its highest and best use, it could be worth as much as $150,000,000, not the $72,000,000 LAUSD estimated. Our argument was that once we got the higher amount in Court, LAUSD would be forced to pay it. They could not walk away. The concept of spending this kind of money or anything like it for a school site was ludicrous and everyone agreed with that except the LAUSD and the politicians it controlled. Even the teacher's union secretly supported us but wouldn't dare take a position against the LAUSD publicly.

We told the legislators, the press and anyone who would listen that if the state allocated the money to the district to take our property, and they condemned us, it was a done deal. LAUSD could not abandon the undertaking because of the harm the condemnation would cause. As it turned out we were wrong. There is nothing the LAUSD cannot do. It held on to our property until the market turned and then abandoned the condemnation claiming that it no longer wanted our property, and demanded back the $47 million bond proceeds which we had used to pay off the underlying loan. At that moment in time, the property could not be sold for even $40 million because the market had turned so bad. Before that turn of events, however, our partnership wasted millions of dollars in legal fees and architectural fees designing a six million square foot project that we could have built as proof of the ultimate value of the land. Our attorneys had done this previously with a very major project in LA and turned a $30 million offer into a $75 million reality. We fully expected to repeat that success. But we could not predict the market turning and the treachery of LAUSD. In time, I had hired the former California District Attorney Ira Reiner to work on this case for us, as well as the eminent Johnnie Cochran who was a terrific guy but he couldn't help us, although we dropped hundreds of thousands on focus groups and mock trials. Scores of meetings, hearings and appeals, left us with nothing. In the end, the partners who were still left, (one had gone under) took Trump out of the deal and went bankrupt. In bankruptcy, they settled the case for a fair amount with LAUSD and the district got its Ambassador. All of this legal wrangling reignited the flame I always had for being a lawyer. It also inspired me to take a position on my local school board, which I held for six years.

Chapter 15 – My Epiphany

On this particular day I had business in the office of an engineer in NJ who was working the Paramus project for me. I remember being in the elevator with him when the subject of the Thomas hearings came up. It was a Friday. This engineer was a man I liked a lot because he was a very good person. But he had not had the best of experiences with his wife, and despite his regard and respect for me, I would have to categorize him as somewhat of a sexist. He was also a political conservative. We must have passed a television or some kind of news report might have been playing that prompted him to make an offhand crack about the "bitch" who was making accusations against Clarence Thomas, the nominee for Supreme Court Justice, and the trouble she was stirring up at his confirmation hearings.

I knew that the great Thurgood Marshall was being replaced on the Bench. I hated George Bush, ever since the time he debated Geraldine Ferraro, one of my personal heroes and on whose finance committee for NY Senate, I would later serve. Bush acted like a total jerk and his obvious contempt and disrespect for Ferraro warned me, long in advance, that this was not a person who was interested in promoting women's rights or interests. So when he nominated Thomas, I immediately expected that the he was an "Uncle Tom" who would march in lockstep with the Bush administration's repressive policies and do his part to twist the constitution to support anti-abortion, anti-equal opportunity positions. It was not something I was particularly focused upon except to know I opposed this guy Thomas, but it made no difference at all what he stood for, because no one in the Senate would have the courage to deny a black man this seat, no matter what he had done or whatever lack of qualification he demonstrated.

However, I knew nothing about a bitch stirring things up. Suddenly I was interested. I remember getting into my car that afternoon and putting on the hearings on the radio. I listened in the car and then walked into my house and turned on the television. From that moment on I was transfixed.

The subject of sexual harassment became a national issue. But this was nothing new to me. I understood it from the inside out, I just never heard it discussed so openly and rationally. Of course, in return, I was forced to watch the likes of Alan Simpson, Arlen Spector and Orrin Hatch systematically punish the victim exhibiting the very type of the behavior they professed to abhor. On the news, and in print, people were talking more about sexual harassment than the two individuals at the heart of the controversy, and, were it not for Thomas's later horrible record on the Bench, I might have said it was worth appointing him just to get the subject out in the open.

Alan, Arlen and Orrin - the three inquisitors. That is how I came to know them for those days and beyond. Years later, I was lunching at a fancy eatery in LA when Orrin Hatch walked in with that little guy who was a studio head and ran the motion picture academy for a while. I looked Hatch in the eye and gave him a death stare. I hated him as much at that moment as I do now and as I did on October 13, 1991. I never saw Spector face to face but I remember how the specter of Spector cross-examining Hill served to raise consciousness across the country about the double standard women were living with at the hands of the likes of him.

It's ironic that when you google the Thomas hearings you inevitably come up with something like the Hill-Thomas hearings as if Anita Hill was up on a charge, or as the case with Thomas, for a confirmation hearing. But Alan, Orrin and Arlen did put her on trial. Not a real trial where the rules of evidence were followed, or the rules of common decency, for that matter. It was more like a witch hunt. Hill had to pay for telling the truth about Thomas. But punishing her was not enough to resurrect the potential appointment of Thomas, Hill would have to be discredited, and to do that she would have to be dragged through the mud, falsely accused, tried and hung. Who better than Alan, Arlen and Orrin for the job?

The question of whether or not Hill was telling the truth really doesn't matter so much as the issue of what she raised as improper behavior. Many people, or, I should say, men, reacted to her allegations with "So what?" This ubiquitous reaction gave rise to the expression, "They just don't get it", which by the way, they didn't, as was the case with my friend, the engineer. It would take years for many men to be able to understand what makes a hostile environment and what the effect of that can be. Sadly, many still deny that this occurs.

In 1991, sexual harassment was rampant in the workplace yet many people didn't know it was even wrong, much less had a name. The creation of a "hostile environment", first established in the Supreme Court case "Meritor" or the concept of gender discrimination from "Price Waterhouse" were kicking around in legal circles but they were hardly household words. But most women who had held jobs had a good understanding of what it meant, even if they didn't know the name. And most women who worked had been victimized to one degree or another whether they paid a high emotional price like myself, or were just angered by the fact that a man doing exactly the same work was getting paid significantly more. You would be hard pressed to find a woman in 1991 who was not the victim of some form of sexual harassment or discrimination. Unfortunately for me, I was a veritable "poster child."

In 1991, I was 42 years old. I had accomplished much, earned a hell of a lot of money, and had two incredible children. There was nothing about me that would lead the casual viewer to suspect that the Thomas Hearings would have such a profound effect. But I was the original harassee, at least from my point of view, and I had blocked much of my experience, allowing it to change me, harden me and punish me for a for the only crime of which I was guilty – being a woman. All of this repressed memory came back over the three days of Thomas hearings and the days and weeks that followed.

When you are 21, and you have to walk around in an atmosphere where there a pictures of naked woman all around you, you need to make some adjustments. By this age, I had already grown to hate Playboy magazine. I knew that these pictures reinforced the madonna whore double standard, set up women to impossible to achieve levels of beauty and worst of all reduced them to sex objects at the same time. (I later came to realize that the proliferation of women as sexual beings did something to advance the sexual freedom of all women, but at what price? I am still debating the net sum of this in my mind today, and I think it is positive. But much of the positive effect has to do with society in general, changes in thought and approach reflected in literature and other cultural medium such as television, that makes me certain that I do not have to worry about crediting Hugh Hefner for any of this progress. So the internal debate goes on, and I will never reach a conclusion.)

Whether nudies ultimately helped advance the sexual independence of women or not is irrelevant to what they did to me, which was in all aspects negative. When I first started at Zwicker Electric, and throughout my time in the construction business working in the field and even the office, these pictures were everywhere, and this is how the men felt about it: Some men wanted them removed so that my delicate virginal feelings would not be hurt. Some men said that if I wanted to work in a field I didn't belong in, I should have to expect to confront these objects which were totally appropriate to this "men only" environment. Some men perversely enjoyed the discomfort they expected these pictures to cause me and exploited that by pointing out the existence of the pictures, even going so far as to confront me with statements like, "I bet you wish you looked like her," or "You remind me of Miss April, but her hair is darker." And some men used the atmosphere to remind me of my place in the world, and in that office, in particular, was as an object of men's desire, put on earth to procreate and serve.

I tried not to let it bother me. I convinced myself that it didn't bother me. I changed myself to blunt its effects. And I cried.

I think I first noticed that sexual intimidation had an effect on me when I started taking up cursing. I grew up in an environment where using the word. "damn" got you soap in the mouth. When I was 18, I worked as a part time assistant in my sister's office, during my two week winter recess from college. I was happy for the job helping with the filing and typing. My sister was an old fashioned Executive Secretary, which means she did the work of an Assistant Vice President along with typing and answering the phone and received a quarter of the pay. Having said that, she was very well paid for the time for a secretary and highly respected. What was strange and appalling was the speech in her office. We are talking about the ivory tower here, not some field shanty, but everything was fuck fuck fuck. I was totally shocked. I wanted to hide whenever one of the bosses went off on a tirade. I didn't know how Elaine and the other woman in the office were able to handle this. I never said the work fuck in my life and did not expect to. When I heard it, I thought sexual intercourse, and it embarrassed me. I was probably red in the face for the entire two weeks.

Eventually, I would become known for my foul mouth. I was the proverbial sailor, cursing with the best of them. Actually, better than the best of them. And there was a reason for this. When I finally started working in the field, one of the objections men voiced about me, one of the reasons I didn't "belong" was that my presence hampered them from talking freely, cursing as it were. Of course this is total bullshit, or what we lawyers call a pretext. I chose to adapt my language to that of the field because it was the most expeditious thing to do. I just started to talk like them, even though it was totally alien to me. I suppressed my embarrassment, and went with the flow, the end result was I managed to eliminate one of the excuses why I shouldn't be in the field, but it opened the door to criticism of me as a potty mouth. Sort of a no win situation. There were two types of women when it came to anything. In this case, refined women and slobs. I fell into the latter category. So I gave up a part of my identity to be one of the boys and it cost me, but it also helped me get along in the field.

There is no way to counter sexual intimidation. For instance, what could I possibly do when I was walking a construction site where construction workers regularly peed on the bare columns, and someone decided to take a leak? Walk away? Frequently that decision was directly related to my appearance on the scene. Is there a person alive who would think I should drop my pants and pee too? Rhetorical question, but it points out the inequality in the situation. What I ended up doing was go on with my business. I learned to ignore the pee takers, but again with a price. Peeing on columns has an interesting history. I think it is a form of machismo, and men do it in front of each other as well. Imagine the thought that the concrete floor behind a decorative column, trimmed in leather or elegant wood, in a fine office or a luxury apartment, has been flooded with piss. When we turned on the heat at Trump Tower, the smell of piss was unbearable. We had to fumigate around the columns where the fan coil units were located. There are always portable potties on a job site, it is the law. Yet, they pee on columns. Imagine the burst of testosterone when you can pee on a column in front of a woman who just happens to be there. Yes, I ignored it. So they couldn't say that I inhibited the normal act of an ordinary construction worker. But they could say, "go ahead and whip it out in front of Barbara, she likes it." And they did.

The biggest personal accommodation I made had to do with having kids. I can't say I ever thought much about having children, but I certainly was never opposed to it. I imagine that I expected I would just have a family like everyone else. I even had a girl's name picked. I would call her Julie after my aunt Julia, the nun, who I perceived as an early feminist with limited choices. Julia wanted to work her entire life, and probably did not want to have children. She chose the convent which was a viable option for so many nurses, teachers and other skilled educated women and it was an occupation that was extremely well respected. Being a nun allowed a woman to pursue a career without being called a spinster or a shrew, or a dyke for that matter. My Aunt Julia was an x-ray technician at St. Joseph's hospital in Rockaway. She was so devoted to her work that it eventually cost her her life. She over exposed herself to radiation by not wearing her monitor all the time. She worked far more hours than she should have. She died of cancer. But while she lived, she was my favorite aunt and very liberal, often convincing my mother to be more permissive with me than she might have been inclined. Having picked a name, I guess I expected to at least have a girl sometime.

When I started working people thought I was a novelty. I was an engineering student and a girl. But the moment I became a wife, I was seen as a potential baby factory and the fact that I even wanted to work was proof that I was infertile, to the kindly people, and not a real woman to the rest, who viewed me as lacking in the natural instinct of wanting to be a mother, which they saw as the only role in life for a woman. So I fought this. And it was a fight. One of the people who pushed me hardest on this was my brother in law, Vic Lappe. He convinced me that I could not have both a job and a family. This was a very smart man, brilliant, as a matter of fact, and I honestly do not believe he meant to do any harm, as I often felt that others who persecuted me had no idea of what they were doing. When I confronted some of my tormenters in the aftermath of the Thomas hearings, they all insisted that they meant no harm, but that rang hollow. What was the point of saying a woman can't have a job, especially in construction, and babies too? Just another way of saying that men are superior to women. Another barrier to equality.

Meanwhile, my sister was pushing me hard to have kids. She even offered to take care of them for me. People at work, as well as family, asked me when I was going to have children. I was inclined to say, why? So you can fire me? Back in the day, you could be fired for having a child. You could be "not hired" for being of childbearing age and it was perfectly legal. When a couple applied for a mortgage on a home, the wife's income was routinely not considered in the calculations of what amount to lend because it was assumed that she would have a child and not contribute to the payments. Working with a child and a husband was not a possibility to consider. It was a given that women had children stayed at home. It was a cultural truism.

I think for the entire 1970's I was looked upon as a ticking pregnancy time bomb, but after a while, most people assumed that I was infertile and the pressure let up. But here's what really happened to me. I became convinced that I could not have children and still keep my job. None of this was conscious, but unconsciously, I knew that I was making the choice of work over kids. I was beginning to really excel at what I was doing and wanted to run with it. I knew a lot of married women, mostly as the wives of my co-workers and family, because I had very few women friends and none of them had children. A lot of the women I knew resented me, but mostly they just didn't like the idea of me, that I was working in a man's world. As much as feminism had done to empower women, there was a class of women who it had inadvertently alienated, that is, women who had chosen to have children and who could afford not to go to work. So a quiet war started between working mothers and non-working mothers. I was staying clear of that mess by not having children. I convinced myself that I didn't want them, although I doted on my nieces and nephews and really adored children all my life. But I actually went through a period where I felt I mustn't have a child period and got used to it. It was easy to convince myself that if I had a child it would be the end of my career and life as I knew it. I reached a point where I did not want a child. As much as I encountered resentment and criticism from the stay at home moms, I experienced a tremendous disdain for women who had chosen to "give up their lives." Although I no longer disrespect women who chose not to work outside of the house, I still believe that it important to society that both parents function not only in their child rearing roles, but play a role, no matter how minor, in the nation's industry. By choosing to stay at home, women continue to reinforce the prejudices against working women that I suffered.

When I finally became pregnant, (by supernatural intervention I always say), I was shocked to be happy. But I was extremely defensive and scared. For one thing, I wouldn't tell anyone I was pregnant until after I had the amniocentesis. Of course, my husband blabbed it to the entire family, which was OK because I would have told them anyway, but I worked hard to keep the news out of the industry. Unfortunately, I took a trip to Europe for business and told one of my travelling companions because I thought it was unsafe for me to travel without anyone knowing it. Forget it, within a week the news was all over – it spread like wildfire. And what were people saying? That I would quit work! In one fell swoop, a simple pregnancy was sufficient to wipe out all that I had accomplished in 14 years of fighting my way up the ladder in a male dominated industry. That's how much they thought of me! Of course, I didn't quit.

I punished myself in the beginning by not allowing myself to enjoy my pregnancy but after word got out and I had no secrets I just eased into my role and I loved being pregnant. Of course, I did it my way, meaning I worked just as hard as I ever did, and I downplayed the maternal role way too much. I should not have done that, but again, I was proving myself as engineer over woman. I remember being asked about how I was going to work full time when I had a baby keeping me up at night. Of course, this was just more goading. More harassment. But instead of saying fuck you, like I would now, I capitulated by denying my own instincts and saying I would have a nanny as if I didn't even care to be a mother and having a kid was just another job for me.

Being pregnant with twins at my age made me high risk. Throughout the entire pregnancy my doctor tried to get me to quit work. He could not conceive of why I wanted to stay on the job and earnestly asked me if my husband was working and did I need the money. Telling him that I was in charge of the construction of a major project in New York that was in excavation was pointless. In a way, I guess he was right. I have always put my work ahead of my personal life. I worked the day my kids were born. I wasn't feeling well and went to the doctor. He took one look at me and said that was it, I had to quit. That night I was beside myself. I didn't plan to quit necessarily, but I knew I would have to take off at least the next day, and there was an important meeting I had to make. I was more worried about missing a goddamned meeting than my own health. My water broke and I was taken to the hospital. My twins were born 10 weeks premature. I was back at work in a week. Until the Thomas hearings, I never realized how I let the world almost deprive me of what I value most in my life.

Sexual intimidation, discrimination, being forced to live in a hostile environment, endless harassment and being measured against expectations based solely on gender stereotypes shaped me from the time I started engineering school until that day in October. It made me tough and it made me crass. It almost stopped me from being a mother. It convinced me that I had to make choices when I did not have to make them. I always laugh at the notion of "having it all". Women can have it, women can't have it. I used to say that if you define having it all as having kids and a job then I suppose most men in the world have it all – why aren't they happier?

It turns out that having it all really means having what you deserve. Being free and equal and being allowed to live in an environment where you are protected to the extent possible from intimidation and hostility. Just as the government insures safety to workers who labor in hazardous industries, it can and must insure protection to women who work period. The Meritor and Price Waterhouse cases helped a lot to enforce laws that were routinely ignored but it was the Thomas hearings that forced Americans to confront sexual harassment and do something about it.

I was different after Thomas. First, I was angry. My son who was only 6 years old at the time, reminded me when I asked him recently if he remembered the senate hearings on TV, by telling me that he recalled that I told him and his sister that it was very important, and that I was very angry about what was going on. I was angry for a long time. I was disgusted at the idea that Thomas was confirmed, and he continues to disgust me with his deportment on the Bench. I was disgraced by the conduct of the Republican partisans and their willingness to engage in stereotyping Anita Hill. Most of all I was sickened by the conduct of the likes of Biden and Kennedy and the other Democrats who were willing to saddle this country with an inferior Supreme Court Justice, out of either fear of going against a black man, or more likely out of lack of willingness to go out on a limb for a woman's rights issue. The latter is true, I am sure, and if you need confirmation, all you need to do is think about how Obama became our president rather than the more deserving Hillary Clinton. Now, as ever, there are still barriers, prejudices and resentments that women encounter in every path on every day. Ironically, the Clinton campaign demonstrated just how acceptable discrimination still is. So called enlightened liberals talked about Hillary's physical characteristics as if they were boys in the locker room. La plus ca change, la plus c'est la meme chose.

  As the anger subsided, the memories came flooding in. They came back not as shadows of the past but as if they were real. I was reliving my memories. I could visualize guys laughing at me as I walked past someone on the jobsite who just had to take a leak right out in the open the minute

I showed up. I relived being in an elevator crammed with 30 men, when an electrician said to me, "Barbara, I hear you give good head." I relived seeing sketches of me on stairway walls with my legs spread open. I relived seeing all the photographs – the gynecological ones you find in Penthouse, plastered on the toolboxes. They said, if I wanted to walk into the shanties, then I deserved to have to see the pictures. Because it was the pictures that belonged, not me. Most of all, and worst of all, I realized why it took me so long to have my children and I shuddered at the thought that it might not have happened at all.

    I started making phone calls. Remember, I was a biggish shot now, not some girl trying to do a man's job. I called the head of an engineering company and confronted him with the fact that he once walked into a meeting filled with men, not just workers but architects and engineers and said, "if you pick up her skirt, you'll see Barbara has a pair of balls under there." First he denied ever having said that. Then without admitting it, he said it was a compliment. He said he was saying that I was strong and forceful. This is the "they don't get it" part. He actually thought that he could get away with telling me that it is a compliment to a woman to say she has a pair of balls. What does that mean? That women without balls, obviously all women except me, are less than men? What about the overtly sexual reference to picking up my skirt (of course, I never wore a skirt to work)? What about discussing testicles in mixed company, that is, 20 men and one woman. I was merciless to him. And he was doing work for me at the time, so I had power over him too. And, in the end, that is what it is all about.

Someone said, "Men use sex to maintain power in the workplace." This is as good a starting point as any to explain what sexual harassment is. Like rape, sexual harassment has very little to do with sex. It has taken people a long time to realize that a person who forces another to have sex is not doing it for want of sex. He is doing it to overpower the other, to control her (him). That is my very simple understanding of a complicated subject. I am grateful to say that I have never experienced rape nor has anyone I know. But, I humbly say I wrote the book on sexual harassment.

In law school I had an argument with a female student over a vignette I related. I told the class I had one boss who greeted the men with hello or a handshake but always gave me a boob crushing hug. The student did not understand how this could possibly be sexual harassment. She even said that in many cultures it is necessary or appropriate to do this. She obviously missed the relationship between culture and discrimination and the cultures she chose to mention were those particularly known to treat women unequally. But maybe this is not harassment. I suppose it depends on the circumstances. Americans tend to poo poo hugging with like sexes but opposites is fine. Who initiated the hug? Was it a "I haven't seen you for a while, or you are a close friend, or sorry about your dead dog hug"? Imagine that a man hugs a women he doesn't know at all. Or partly knows. Or knows only as well as he knows the men he is shaking hands with. What the hell is a hug about? Even if he knows her very well, do the others know that? Isn't it true that by acting this way, especially as the boss, that he is saying you are different. Now, if it's me being hugged, I probably don't care about it, and if I don't like it, I will make myself heard. But what about a partner and a 2nd year associate? She takes the hug. And everyone sees her take the hug. There are so many permutations to this I could go on forever. Is the crowd mixed? What are the circumstances of the meeting?

A real life example: Clarence Thomas asks Anita Hill if she likes porno movies. Do you know how many times I have been asked that? - Does she know anything about bestiality? I know about it. I have been shown pictures of it just to get a rise out of me. I have been invited to engage in all sorts of unusual acts. The kind Anita Hill got to hear about. But, why ask the question in the first place? Do you really want to know if I like porno? Do you really think I want to hear a dirty joke? Do I want to be embarrassed? In front of a crowd of men? Do I want to go out with you? What do you think? I think you want to put me in my place!

The truth is, I am sickened and repulsed by you. As was Anita Hill. Well, why did she stay in touch with him then? Why didn't she report him? Didn't she keep calling him? Didn't she really want him? Is she making this up? Why would a *normal* woman put up with this?

*Because **I** did it, goddammit, I did it. I followed my tormenters like a dog, I waited for them to beat me again, I took it, I let it happen, I was even almost convinced that I deserved for it to happen. And I needed them. They had my future in their hands. They had the power. They had the control. Yes, I kept going back because there was nowhere else to go. I know what it's like to have to kiss the ass of someone who's fucking you over.*

I sat there transfixed watching Professor Hill being questioned as if it were me. I felt the disdain and derision heaped on her, and I felt her shame. I heard her called names and written off as a quack desperate for the affection of a man who made her life a living hell, and I cried.

I am moving steadily toward coming to terms with all of this. I will never be the innocent kid that just liked Math, but got herself mixed up in the wrong business. I will always have to strain to keep my language appropriate in public and I will still get looked down upon for the potty mouth I can't seem to shake. I will always wish I had more kids. People, especially young women will grow weary listening to me. Some will discredit what I have to say. And there will always be that thread of self doubt. Am I exaggerating, was it really that bad, was it my fault? Then, I will cry a little and feel better knowing that my sacrifices and travails, along with those of many in my generation, have gone to

build an easier road for the women who followed.
A road that remains "under construction".

Chapter 16   The Best Job I Never Had

At a point in time, Roth and I started to go in circles. He did not know exactly what he wanted, he just knew that I was to provide it. I could not get straight direction from him, and he was getting frustrated with my inability to respond. Roth liked to verbally abuse the people who worked for him. He hadn't done this with me, probably because I wasn't there in his office, so he didn't consider me an employee, although I had seen him give it to some of the consultants. Whenever he laid into someone, the appropriate reaction was to remain quiet and let the storm pass. This behavior is antithetical to my nature, so when Roth finally came at me with guns blazing, I gave back worse than I got. I left the office that day and Roth did not call me again. In a few weeks, I knew I was finished with Alexander's. This was in the summer of 1993.

Because I was consulting on the Ambassador Hotel project, I still considered myself an employee of Donald's but I didn't see much of him. So when the invitations went out to his December wedding to Marla Maples, I was very happy to get one. To be honest, I probably owe this to Norma who, no doubt, put my name on the list.

The wedding at the Plaza was, of course, beautiful, and there were about 2,000 people, one more glittering than the other. I remember seeing Howard Stern and OJ Simpson, although there were many more celebrities there. The most important person to me, however, was Steven

Roth. I had not seen or heard from him since our "falling out", and I was hoping for the opportunity to let him know there were no hard feelings on my side. He was there, and we chatted like old friends.

The following week Steve called and asked me to come to his office. He told me he wanted me to work for him and offered me a job at $3000/week. I practically laughed at him. I told him that was an offer I could easily refuse, and anyway, I was still working on the Ambassador and had to go to Los Angeles one or two times a month. He asked me what I wanted. I pulled a number out of the air. $25,000/month as a consultant, and the freedom to work on the Ambassador as needed. He said OK. I almost fell on the floor. I did not expect him to bite. I didn't even know if I wanted the work, but I made an offer and he accepted it, so there I was, in January 1994, working for Steve Roth in Saddle Brook, NJ, the headquarters of his retail empire.

Steve's office was beautiful. He had incredible artwork. In his office, he had a massive paneled painting of a swimming pool by David Hockney. Roth's was the most luxurious office I had worked in. The finishes were all natural top grade everything. The art was all original. He was always bringing new things into the office, some of them outrageous. I remember he had some colorful sculptures of bodybuilders with an acrylic like finish, that I thought were hideous but they were probably valued in the hundreds of thousands. Roth's wife was a Broadway producer and I am sure she had a hand in the decorating. Donald talked about class, but he was about copies. Roth was all about the real thing.

Steve liked me especially for my humble beginnings. He said he was on his way to City College himself when his mom got remarried to a wealthy man. Next thing, Roth ended up in Dartmouth, but he never forgot where he came from. There was no sense of pretense about him, but, in fairness to Leonard and Donald, they were not pretentious either. I don't think I would last very long with a phony.

One of the first things I did was rethink the entire Rego Park project. When Alexander's was directly involved in the development, Farkas had a market study done of the area. At the time, street space on nearby Queens Boulevard was getting record high rents, on a parallel with Manhattan. There was a cachement area with a huge apartment population, and also office employees. It was at the intersection of three major thoroughfares, Queens Boulevard, Woodhaven Boulevard and the Long Island Expressway. The income strata for the immediate area justified any kind of retail from your basic Sears up to the high end, just short of the Neiman Marcus variety. In short, it was a retail mecca sitting there just waiting to be exploited. Using an architect that did all of Pyramid's work out of Syracuse that Steve had known, my selection of MEP and structural engineers, I set about getting permission to build a Power Center.

With Rego in full swing, Paramus in development and Lexington Avenue under a magnifying glass, I had a load of work and was extremely happy. My office was great. Steve had an office manager who came in to see me with a decorator and asked me what I wanted to do, the day after I started. The closest I had come to this before was picking out a couch for my office in Trump Tower. I selected a modern style leather couch and chair, and prints of some famous artwork. The desk was already there, but I had to have it modified to add a modesty panel. The office manager ran an ad for a secretary and I got Paula, a terrific young lady, within a few weeks. I asked for a computer, which was supplied immediately, but the office manager told me that Steve could not understand why I would want this. He thought computers were for secretaries. I am sure he has long changed his mind about this. Steve was the first person I knew who had a stock terminal. He knew everything that was going on with the market as it happened.

My relationship with Steve was one of mutual respect, but I was not a snippy with him as I was with Donald, and since I saw him every day, I was a lot closer to him than I was to Leonard. Most of the people in the office were afraid of him and he could yell, but he was overall very generous. Everyone in the office had some kind of stock option. I think Roth liked to be feared.

There were no perks working for Roth in terms of black tie dinners and US Open tickets, but on the whole, it was a nice place to work. It was only a half hour away from my house, there was on site free parking, they had a cafeteria in the building with good food, and as I said, the decorating was beautiful.

As far as atmosphere was concerned, the place was a comedy of sexual harassment. There were four guys, two in leasing, a lawyer and a guy who was a wannabe Roth who considered himself to be in acquisitions, but I always thought he was a short timer. These characters raised dirty talk to an art form. They could not speak without epithets. They talked about women as if they were articles. And this was any women, the women in the office, famous women, women we came across at work. They went into detail about details, this ass, these tits, and for the most part, few women made the grade. Mind you if you took the best characteristics each of these jokers had to offer and made one man, he would still be lacking in looks and personality. It was so far out there, it was surreal. I couldn't take it seriously because it was too over the edge. No one took them seriously. I had a picture of me from the old days on my desk one day and the self important one saw it. He reacted to it by telling me I was "doable". Doable? I would do you? Not in a million fucking years I told him.

The funny thing was no one really cared about this. There were normal men in the office and several women. Some of the women mixed it up and others not, but they all thought these guys were just harmless jerks, and some of the stuff they said and did was actually funny. One man, in particular, the lawyer, was self-deprecating and very original, often drop dead hysterical. I inquired among the women if they wanted me to do anything about the harassment, which I could have, but no one seemed to care. They were not threatened because, within this particular environment, everyone understood his or her respective role. Outside the environment, these few dopes were particularly quiet, especially around Roth, and I suspected if he knew what was going on he would have put a stop to it. It was a very interesting study in human nature and adaptation. I think in the short form, the lack of respect these men got from Roth was compensated for by their shenanigans. I earnestly think they thought they were not hurting anyone and to a limited degree, they were not. Ultimately, they were hurting themselves by not living up to societal norms on a regular basis. Taken from the enclave, none of them would be capable of having a normal office interplay with coworkers and would probably become loners.

  I didn't have very much business interaction with these people, but I often took a stroll around the office, and being a very sociable person, I got quite involved. After a while I started having lunch with them and I was probably the highest ranking member of the group, or tied with the lawyer. It was like sleeping with the enemy. Other than being totally vile and obscene, they were nice guys.

  The more important people with whom I interacted were very conservative and were pretty silent around Roth. If he did not ask a question, no one volunteered anything. This was a whole new management style for me and I didn't like it. In time, I grew to realize that these guys were just avoiding confrontation. They knew their jobs and they did them very well. Unlike me, they had much thicker skins, and conversely, not quite the courage to take Steve on.

    I was really enjoying my work and felt we were making good progress. One of the things that took a bit of work was getting Steve to accept the fact that people in New York would park in a multistory garage. He was a power retail man. All the parking was in front of the building on street level. That was the suburbs. He needed to understand that we were in New York City and city shoppers were different. There were two major retail centers near our site. One was a standalone Macys, (where I used to work) that had the retailer's biggest numbers in the country, except for Herald Square, and they had indoor parking. Then there was Queens Center that had indoor parking with tricky double helixes that are hard to maneuver. But they also had great retail and people in NYC are used to making the most of small places. This was a very successful mall, tricky parking notwithstanding. Finally assured that they could be operated safely and efficiently, Roth went along with the parking deck notion. We were ready to go on Rego Park. I hired York Hunter, a general contractor to be our construction manager.

Roth was particularly interested in doing something with the Lexington Avenue site. We were looking at various configurations when, out of nowhere, the Port Authority announced it was going to build a rail connector to Kennedy airport and was interested in condemning our site via eminent domain to use as the point of entry. Roth and I spent a lot of time talking with the PA people and I learned about their plans for snaking its train through the borough of Queens, condemning everything in its way. Even I knew that the cost of such a venture was beyond the government's coffers. But we had to work with them and we did. In the meantime, Roth was talking to Sotheby's about moving its headquarters to the site. Of course, we would do a super high rise with office as well. Whether it was as flashy as Trump's plans didn't really matter. It would be exciting!

The stock Donald owned had been taken over by Citibank and the head of Citibank was friendly with Irving Fisher of HRH Construction. Very uncharacteristically, Citibank started communicating to Roth a desire to participate in the development. This was a tactic, and Roth knew it. Roth played hardball with the best. He was not going to be questioned or challenged by people that had no concept of development, especially retail development, when Roth himself was the master. No way was he "partnering" on the oversight of his developments.

He decided to go for broke and he told Citibank "OK, you go do it." Go lease it, build it out and open it. Citibank had HRH waiting in the wings to "take over". The concept of anyone at HRH running a development was farfetched to me, but this was a bare knuckled game, and Citibank had enough to make a play. For all intents and purposes, Citibank claimed it could come in and complete the development of all the sites without Roth's involvement at all. Since I worked for Roth, and not Alexander's anymore, this had an enormous impact on my standing.

Here is how I found all this out: My son was in the hospital recuperating from surgery. I was at his bedside. I got a call from my husband saying I needed to call the office, it was urgent. It turned out that Joel Silverman from HRH was looking for me - it was an emergency. I called Joel, whom I had been good friends with since college. Joel was an officer at HRH and when I finally reached him, he told me that HRH was now officially in charge of all development for Alexander's and they were going to build out Rego Park and let York Hunter, the contractor I had hired and was working with, go. HRH was also going to be in charge of the other projects from that point on. He wanted to give me a heads up so I wouldn't be caught surprised.

Forget it, I was devastated. I spoke to Roth about it and he told me that was the way it had to be. He knew what he was doing and I appreciated that, but from my point of view, I was out of a job. The last thing, I mean the very last thing I was ever going to do was to have to answer to HRH. Joel was my friend, but there were people there that I could not work with, let alone for. Roth wanted me to stay on, but doing what? He had a more than capable architect who supervised all of the retail work in the dozens of strip shopping centers he owned in several states. If HRH needed anyone to push around, they could try him. Roth did not need my help with his strip mall projects. Plus, I was a high rise person, or at least a complicated project person. There was nothing for me without the Alexander's projects - that is why he hired me.

I realize now that Steve was playing a waiting game and he was willing to keep me around for the wait. But to me, I was not going to sit on my hands, especially if there was any chance I would end up being let go. My ego couldn't take that any more than it could take working under HRH. I had no idea that it was all a bluff in a game of high stakes poker and Roth understandably couldn't let me in on the strategy. I told Roth that it was not fair to him to have me be doing nothing, and it was not fair to me. His offer was generous but I could not accept it. I would be leaving at the end of the following week.

As it turned out, my last day was the day of the Vornado Christmas party. It was a very nice affair that was held in a fancy restaurant in Hackensack, to be followed, as rumor had the tradition, by an unofficial second party at a local hotel. At the official party, Steve Roth made a speech. He spoke about the status of the company, encouraging and rallying the troops and promised the entire staff that if the stock reached a certain price, he would take everyone and their spouses to Bermuda. Roth was incredibly generous with his people, and he had done this before so he his word was golden.

Then, to my shock and surprise, he turned the subject of his speech to me. He said that I was probably the highest paid woman in New Jersey, which was preposterous, but I think he really believed what I made was a lot of money for a woman. Then he went on to say that I was crazy to give up this job but that I had more integrity than any one he knew. Wow. Then he wished me luck.

I will always remember that party. And the after party. We all went to a Marriott and proceeded to get ridiculously drunk. I partied hearty with the jerks, and the non-jerks, and had a terrific time. By the time I was ready to go, I was fairly hammered.

When I drove home, I stayed in the right lane all the way. This was a big departure for me, to play it safe. But I figured I had the rest of my life to take chances.

THE END

Epilogue

There is no question in my mind that had I remained with Roth I would have had the opportunity to work on the most challenging projects, and would likely have become quite wealthy. But there was no telling how long I would have been just sitting around collecting dust and I chose not to do that. Plus, it was true that had some personal matters to attend to and I was plenty busy with the case in Los Angeles. During the following years, I billed a very livable salary to that project, although the work was different from what I had done in my career previously, more legal than anything else, so much so that after a session with the Mayor of Los Angeles, he asked me what law school I attended. The choice to leave Roth ended my high flying glamour days and ultimately impacted my world view and my position in it.

Dealing with the LAUSD sparked my interest in education and I spent several years on my local school board at home. I like to think I was influential in some areas. I was a big proponent of spending money on technology when it was a new thing in the public school system. I also put myself out on a limb fighting for the elimination of homogeneous grouping of students, a practice that I consider barbaric. I won that fight but took several personal hits for my trouble, as did my children. The good thing is that low performing students are no longer singled out and doomed to the self-fulfilling prophesies that are usually leveled upon them. This may be one of the major contributions I have made in my life.

During these few years, I had quite a bit of time to spend with my children and I watched them grow up into the magnificent adults they are today. Intentionally, or inadvertently, I impacted their world views on things like human rights and basic freedoms. Instead of socking money away in the bank, we spent much of ours taking our children to the four corners of the world, educating them in a way that cannot occur in a classroom. Being raised poor led both my husband and myself to value money in a very different way. We wanted to make certain that, unlike ourselves, our kids had everything they wanted. The end result of this treatment was not spoiled children but honest, liberal, understanding children who appreciate the value of work yet disdain the use of net worth as a yardstick by which to measure the value of individuals. Money is for having, spending or saving, as one sees fit. It cannot be used to define a person's worth, character or class.

The California partners who had brought in Donald wanted to declare bankruptcy rather than let the school board take the Ambassador. It took some doing but they managed to unleash Donald and then successfully pursued a legal course that included bankruptcy and required a viable development plan that would prove the property had a value in excess of what the district had put up. Ultimately the partners pulled their money, and then some, out of the Ambassador site and

LAUSD went on to build its first new high school in almost 40 years, and its biggest debacle, the most expensive school in the world. I remained with the project for a time after Donald left but since the entire nature of the endeavor had changed dramatically, I didn't really see a need for me, and I began to think the partners agreed with that sentiment.

In the fall of 1999, I took a job with a company called Club Quarters, to head up all of their facilities and construction in the United States and Europe. They were a small but rapidly growing membership only hotel group with big plans for the future and promises to match them. The work was grueling. It seemed as if I was on a plane every day. What we did was mostly restoration work, but I built a ground up building in San Francisco. Working beyond New York City was a true eye opener. The concept of building a concrete building on a two or even three day cycle was totally alien to outsiders. They could not imagine it and thought I was making it up. If a job took a year in NY, it took 18 months in San Francisco, maybe only 15 in Chicago. New York construction workers are a different breed of cat, keeping pace with the fast moving city.

The hardest project I ever worked on was the renovation and restoration of the Mather Building on Wacker Drive, in Chicago which was once, for a very brief moment in time, the tallest building in the world. This building had dropped so much material from its top that the streets had to be closed down. It was in total decay with only a few straggler office tenants and Club Quarters got it for almost nothing. The owners decided to leave the few remaining tenants in the building and that made the construction that much harder. They should have paid them off and got rid of them. Another mistake the owners made was to fire the engineering staff. Without them, keeping the building functional was almost impossible. Club Quarters was virulently anti-union and since the building had been run by union engineers, there was no discussion. I ended up having to rely on the mechanical contractor I hired to figure out how to keep the old stuff working until it was replaced. We had only two operating elevators and one was supposed to be reserved for the tenants. The other was carrying men and materials up as far as the 36th floor. Unfortunately one or the other would break down. The office tenants tied up half the time of the construction project manager with their complaints.

We rebuilt the top of the building by making an aluminum copy of the original terra cotta cupola and flew it, in pieces, over the Chicago River to rest on the top of the steel structure. That made all the Chicago papers. This building won awards and big tax credits for the restoration.

We created rooms where there were no rooms and extended the elevators up two floors to serve them. Then we made hotel rooms out of empty office floors, brought the building up to code and provided totally new mechanical services. I spent many hours conferring and cajoling building and fire department officials to make that happen. We did this with a backdrop of very demanding tenants who were impossible to satisfy or shut up. The city of Chicago closed Wacker drive for its own repairs and we lost our entrance. Everyone and everything had to go through the basement. Kudos to all the construction workers on this site, it was pure hell.

I did two Chicago projects, and one in London, which was the easiest of all the Club Quarters jobs because, given the differences in the way contracts are bought out and ultimately built, the contractor virtually gets to dictate the budgets and the schedule and they gave themselves plenty of room. I watchdogged those contractors, along with our excellent engineers, Lehr Associates, who were on site every day to prevent the contractors from building an inferior building, which is often the case when Americans build in Europe.

The project in San Francisco was to be a new poured in place concrete structure on a pile foundation. The job required demolishing some buildings that were built on the landfill that was added when the city was enlarged. We became aware that under the existing structures was a sunken ship. Fortunately only a small part would be exposed and so there was no need for a salvage attempt. As we excavated for the basement, we quickly learned that we were misinformed about the location of the ship and we were going to unearth the entire thing. Now we would have to deal with preservationists. The job was stopped in its tracks.

While hired gun lawyers and archaeologists argued the merits of salvaging a 100 year old sunken ship of no historic importance with each other and the city, my job was dying. The contractor and I decided to quietly go ahead with the piles and we drove them right through the ship when no one was looking. Had we not done that, Club Quarters might still be arguing about whether that ship should be salvaged and the project abandoned.

I was always putting out fires in the operating hotels too. A few of the ones built prior to my coming on board had serious problems mainly due to ill-conceived cost savings. For instance, one NY building had to be shut down because of sparks caused by aluminum bus bars with improper copper connections. By substituting aluminum for copper they saved some money. Now that decision had come back to haunt them.

I got hold of an engineer and found an electrician to do the work, all this while I was in San Francisco, trying to make an impossible opening date. Together with a really top notch hotel manager, Tim Dowd, the fix went off without a hitch or complaint. Another time we blew out a few blocks of electrical network in Philadelphia, and I walked the building engineer through replacing the high voltage fuses and getting back online. This was a job I had already saved from a lawsuit by mediating with the contractor who had ditched the project just prior to my arrival at Club Quarters. Everything was a crisis at Club Quarters, because of lack of knowledge, arrogance and impatience. But for the most part, the hotels are well built, clean and safe and I would stay in any one of them.

Working on these hotels was interesting and challenging, and even fun, but the company atmosphere not right. Although I had been separated by time from the sexism and discrimination that dogged me in my early years, this new company was particularly anti-feminist. To this day I cannot be sure why they even hired me except for the prestige my experience with Trump brought to their efforts. They bragged about hiring women, however, for the most part, they were hired because they worked for less money than men in the same jobs, and all of the women they hired fit a prototype reminiscent of the looks/dress/deportment guidelines finally outlawed in the Price Waterhouse discrimination case, years earlier. Although I was a senior executive (the only female VP) and wielded a lot of power and authority, I definitely did not look the way they would have preferred, and, with my construction sensibilities, I was too street smart and not enough corporate. This company was not quite ready for a female with my sense of power, my confidence in what I was doing, and my willingness to protect the project if I thought the direction I received was inappropriate. All the things Nusbaum, Trump and Roth loved about me made the owner of Club Quarters despise me. We parted ways after 4 years, contentiously, with an 8 year lawsuit to follow over the unkept promises I was made when I was hired. Of course, the buildings and my accomplishments remain.

While I took an emotional hit at Club Quarters I learned valuable lessons about work ethic and trust. I took pride in my work and learned, the hard way, to accept the fact that sometimes the only reward or thanks you receive for doing a good job is self realization of having fulfilled your own expectations, or tried your best in so doing. The trust thing is simple - get it in writing, and make it clear. Of course I was jaded when I left Club Quarters, but I have come around to believing in the human race again. Still, I cannot erase the damage the experience did to myself and my family. My family is less forgiving.

After Club Quarters, I got my arbitration business going and attended mediation training and began a consulting business. But personally, I was floundering. The super long hours and endless travel had worn me down emotionally and physically. I needed a break. At the time, both of my kids had just applied to colleges. Julie had taken an early admission and Peter was waiting. It was Christmas and we were all sitting at the dinner table with family talking about the next four years. I was saying how I always wanted to go to law school and should do it while the kids are in college because surely the time will fly by. As a lark, my daughter went to the bookstore the following day and brought me home an LSAT study book with a challenge written on the flap. I picked up the gauntlet.

In February, I took the LSAT and in the summer I was in Law School. One of the very first things I noticed at law school was the sexism. When a woman spoke, she was often ignored. I was shocked at this because there are more women in law school than men. But it was there. I had a conversation with a punk kid once about whether Hillary Clinton could ever run for president. He very proudly boasted that a woman would never be accepted in certain international circles and just could not do the job. I thought I was back in 1971. In one way the jerk was right because Hillary should be our president right now, and she isn't, because, even among democrats, there is still plenty of sex discrimination to go around. On the other hand, the idiot was totally off base about the international element because Hillary turned out to be one of the great Secretaries of State of all time. I discussed this incident with my son Peter and we decided it was the last gasp of a dying breed. This kid was holding on to the ghost of his superiority over women, and he was laughable, not dangerous. My kids are particularly good at divining who the fools are and where the bullshit lies. This will serve them well in life.

I started at Benjamin Cardozo Law School, but transferred a year later to Rutgers. I am a just public school kind of gal. I did well enough at Cardozo, but that school had its own agenda, and was not interested in me or many of the students in my class. Rutgers wanted me and took me right in and it was a decision I never regretted. The students there were as eager and as intelligent, but with an edge that only diversity can bring to a group. The points of view were broader and more liberal. Plus the school was beautiful. I really enjoyed my years in law school, but when I graduated, I was asked to work as Construction Manager by St. Bart's Episcopal Church in New York which was modifying its AC plant and building a restaurant. So I was back in construction. Shortly after that, Pete took on a very good assignment and I decided to try my hand at law. One of the first things I did was take my own lawyers out of their misery and released them from representing me on the Club Quarters law suit. CQ was using insurance funded lawyers to drag this case out hoping the costs would drive me away. My lawyers were working on contingency and had already invested much of their own money and couldn't tolerate all the motions and trial appearances. (This is a very common thing in litigation, the richer side just drains down its adversary. Most lawyers can keep even an expedited case going for years and years. That is why wealthy companies often strike arbitration clauses from contracts when they are dealing with represented parties, because it has time limits. Every developer I worked for struck arbitration from construction contracts to have the control to bleed their opponents to death through legal fees.)

In my case, I had nothing but time. I took over, and ended up engaging in much motion practice, court appearances, wrote a load of briefs, and finally got a settlement that my other lawyer was unable to make happen. In my spare time, I also sued Aetna twice, a stock broker, a doctor, a home improvement store, a juice company and an online travel company. I even argued in the Appellate Division. I did thousands of hours of work on these cases and my settlements hardly covered my costs in time, but the experience and the knowledge was priceless. What I learned in going to court, taking depositions, selecting a jury, arguing motions is not taught in law school. As an associate in a big firm, all I would have done was watched, if I was lucky. Now I have enough experience to represent clients with confidence. I also have a better understanding of the games lawyers and judges play - so much so that I earnestly believe that I could throw out all my ethics books and be better off. Yes, it is an ugly profession at times. Zealous advocacy teeters on the brink of outright dishonesty and often slips over. On one of my cases, I was awarded sanctions against the attorneys, due to the unsavory shenanigans on the other side. But this is something you learn, accept and work around, just like I learned to deal with other adversities I have encountered. I need to find a way to make it work for me. But that way will not involve anything unethical on my part. I am too old to disprove Donald's other charge of "you're too honest.

I recently took a job as interim general counsel of a startup company but I often get the wanderlust for construction, and sometimes think about going back into development. With my legal experience, I am much better prepared to handle the compliance and permitting issues now than I ever was. Then I think I would rather just do straight law and represent clients, preferably construction companies. Of course, I would also like to fight gender discrimination cases but that is a whole other area of law with which I have no experience . . . yet.

Education has become a lifetime commitment for me and I see no end in sight to the improvement of my current skills and the acquisition of new ones. How can I predict the future? All I can say for sure is that whatever comes at me, I am ready. 40 years as a female engineer makes you ready for anything.

Acknowledgements

My son Peter G. Res who is always keeping me on an even keel, edited the book. My daughter Julie Res read the book for inconsistencies and hyperbole, which she does, without even having to ask, for my conversation and other writings. Their contributions to the book and my life are legion.

My sister Elaine Lappe who is my original promoter, supporter and inspiration, fact checked and critiqued the early years.

Several of my friends read the book and provided useful comments: Margaret Rodriquez, Elise Pottick, Arthur Nusbaum, Steven Lawler, Thomas Wells, Julia Read, Louis Maggiotto, Samantha Breslin, Norma Foerderer and Lisa Calandra.

CPSIA information can be obtained at www.ICGtesting.com
Printed in the USA
BVOW06s0110030816

457746BV00011BA/82/P